My Cricket Hero

XII Indians On Their XII Favourite Cricketers

Editor: Gulu Ezekiel

My Cricket Hero

XII Indians On Their XII Favourite Cricketers

Editor: Gulu Ezekiel

Designer: Pragya Srivastava

First published through Amazon KDP in December 2020

Copyright @Gulu Ezekiel, 2020

No part of this book may be reproduced or stored in a retrieval system, or transmitted in any form or by any means, electronic, mechanical, photocopying, recording, or otherwise, without express written permission of the editor

Disclaimer: Every effort has been made to contact copyright holders of material reproduced in this book. We would be pleased to rectify omissions if any in subsequent editions should they be brought to our attention.

Dedicated to

the memory of my

beloved parents

Editor's Introduction

*There are no cricketers like those seen
through 12-year-old eyes. -Ian Peebles*

The germ of the idea of this compilation was planted by the sense of ennui brought on by the dreaded pandemic and long spells of isolation in 2020.

With publishers understandably wary of signing new deals, the best—and only—way out was to self-publish.

This is my first such effort would not have been possible without the co-operation and contributions from all my friends. There was never any hesitation on their part and for that I am extremely grateful.

I wanted the writers to be from a wide range of professions though all with cricket connections. Just two of us are fulltime sports writers—myself and Suresh Menon. The rest encompass the fields of science, books, movies, the law and more.

As I always acknowledge sources, two of the inspirations for the theme of this book is the regular column in *The Cricketer* monthly of UK, 'My Favourite Cricketer' which has been running for many years now a collection of which was brought out in book form in 2010 and *Cricket Heroes* published back in 1984 (*Editor: David Lemmon; Queen Anne Press*). However there were just four Indian cricketers chosen by the contributors in these two books combined and the contributors to *Cricket Heroes* were all cricket writers.

The idea of this book therefore was to get Indians prominent in their fields to choose their favourite Indian cricketers.

It was a lot of fun choosing the contributors and reading their essays and certainly kept the brain cells active and the spirits up during this most challenging time. Hope the readers enjoy this book as much as I did.

--Gulu Ezekiel

New Delhi, December 2020

Photos (Front cover): Polly Umrigar and Vijay Hazare courtesy Pratyush Khaitan Collection. Rest: Gulu Ezekiel collection.

Photos (Back cover): Standing from left: GR Viswanath, Ajay Jadeja and Gulu Ezekiel. Sitting: PR Man Singh and Karsan Ghavri (Gulu Ezekiel collection)

What's Inside

CHAPTER 1
   Polly Umrigar by Keki N. Daruwalla 10

CHAPTER 2
   Chandu Borde by Fredun E. De Vitre 18

CHAPTER 3
   Eknath Solkar by Gulu Ezekiel 30

CHAPTER 4
   Sunil Gavaskar by Hemant Kenkre 36

CHAPTER 5
   Salim Durani by Amrit Mathur 44

CHAPTER 6
   Vijay Hazare by Kersi Meher-Homji 50

CHAPTER 7
   GR Viswanath by Suresh Menon 58

CHAPTER 8
   Kapil Dev by Dr. Narottam Puri 63

CHAPTER 9
   Dilip Sardesai by Rajdeep Sardesai 68

CHAPTER 10
 Tiger Pataudi by Ramesh Sharma 79

CHAPTER 11
 ML Jaisimha by PR Man Singh 88

CHAPTER 12
 Mohinder Amarnath by Karthik Venkatesh . . 95

Epilogue
 Ode to Heroes by Gulu Ezekiel 101

CHAPTER I

Polly Umrigar

by Keki N. Daruwalla

Cricket can be exciting, but only in years does one come across a Test match or a performance calling for minstrels, troubadours, harp and mandolin—sorry I am no scholar on mediaeval music and what instruments they played. But I must boast, that in the Garhwal hills, where I have spent four years, I have seen retired old soldiers, sometimes still in their faded Scottish kilts, entering a valley playing a lone bagpipe, and filling the hills with its music. Would they know what the songs meant—wi'a hundred pipers an'a, an a'?

Did the much-lambasted Polly Umrigar ever enjoy such an occasion? He has been treated meanly by Indian scribes, for that one bad English tour in the English summer of 1952, with Fred Trueman and Alec Bedser in great form, bowling on uncovered pitches awash with rain. Incidentally Trueman spent a winter chopping wood at a friend's farm, to build his muscles. Umrigar had his moments against the West Indian bombers like Wesley Hall and Roy Gilchrist, but was seldom given the credit he deserved.

He was a strong man, six feet tall, broad shouldered, good fielder and could swing his arm, bowling cutters and swing, and also slow off spin. He knew he had just one more Test match to play and then hang up his boots. He was getting on in age and his back was troubling him. He had made up his mind. He was with the Indian team at Queen's Park Oval, Port of Spain, Trinidad for the fourth Test starting April 9, 1962. It had been a bad, eventful tour with the Indian captain Nari Contractor, left hand opening bat, almost killed in a colony game by a lethal delivery by Charlie Griffith whose bowling action was always suspect. Contractor came out alive, an iron plate fixed to his skull, though he never played a Test again.

Polly Umrigar (standing third from left) in the 1941 St. Xavier's College team (Courtesy late Jimmy Wadia)

Young Mansur Ali Khan Pataudi had taken over as captain. His father Iftikar Ali Khan Pataudi had scored a century in the 1932-33 'Bodyline' series and then being a conscientious disapprover of 'Bodyline', as the legend goes, was dropped by captain Douglas Jardine. In 1946, when Pataudi was foolishly elevated as captain, he just scored just 55 runs in three matches.

Umrigar had not been too fluent with the runs, just a single half century in three previous Tests in the 1962 series and a few wickets. Because of the big Indian population, our teams were very welcome in Trinidad, though our cricketers, at least on a first outing, looked only enviously at its rum and Calypso culture. We Indians are diffident to start with.

This was Umrigar's second tour of the Caribbean and in the first in 1953 he had already made his mark, and got the adage 'Palm-tree Hitter.' He had a century in the first Test at Port of Spain and another in the fifth at Kingston, Jamaica.

In the 1962 Test West Indies won the toss, chose to bat and scored 444 for nine declared, aided by a century (139) by Rohan Kanhai, till Umrigar had him lbw. Umrigar took five wickets including those of Conrad Hunte and Kanhai. India were all out for 197, with the devastating Hall mopping up the first five wickets. Umrigar's was the highest score (56) with Pataudi following with 47. These two alone withstood Hall.

With a lead of 247 runs, West Indies asked India to follow on. Salim Durani scored a dashing century, going in one down. Umrigar went in with the score at 192. After that there was mayhem. In the next four hours he hit an unbeaten 172 against Hall, Garry Sobers and all out of 230 runs scored. If Neville Cardus could think of Alexandre Duma's D'artaganan talking of a batsman, here he would have needed Athos, Porthos and Aramis, all three to cast a reflection on the innings.

Mankad had at Lords, scored 72 in the first innings and

then taken five wickets before that 184 which brought him laurels. The skies seemed to rain superlatives. It was recognised as one of the great all-time feats in the history of the game. Umrigar's was just a fraction less. 172 instead of 184, 56 instead of 72. Both got five wickets. What did Mihir Bose in his *A History of Indian Cricket* have to say of the performance? "Even Umrigar. who had only twice reached 50 in the series, now attacked boldly, making 172 not out of 230 in 248 minutes."

That's all, one short throwaway sentence in a 571-page book. We can be niggardly, can't we?

Those were tough days. Forget thighpads, elbow guards, helmets, referrals and often uncovered pitches. Payments were niggardly; an unknown IPL cricketer from the wilds would smile at the kind of money on offer. And playing in Pakistan, one had to deal with Pakistani umpires. Pahlan Ratanji Umrigar was a bridge between the likes of CK Nayudu andLala Amarnath of the 1930s and the Vijays—Merchant, Hazare and Manjrekar who were too defensive. He seldom threw his wicket away. Yet he hit his sixes with abandon, when in full flow. His pulls, square cuts and straight drives were a delight to watch. He was never a stylist like Rusi Modi or ML Jaisimha. His hits were robust, power-packed, making a din as the ball hit the rails.

In March 1960 I went from Meerut to watch the Irani Cup match at the Railways stadium in Delhi. Umrigar had scored about 60 runs by lunch, fairly sedately for Bombay v Rest of India. While people were getting back to their seats, in the first over after lunch he hit four boundaries. Then he marched to his century without any fireworks. That was Umrigar, a mix of daredevilry with responsibility.

As a boy of 11, I had missed watching him in the first Test at Feroz Shah Kotla in 1948. He was in the 12, but Amarnath chose Keki Tarapore, aged 40, for the only Test he ever played. Umrigar had hit a century for the Combined Universities team against West Indies. The Windies scored

631 after an initial collapse engineered by CR Rangachari. He had got Allan Rae, Jeffrey Stollmeyer and George Headley, once known as the 'Black Bradman', in a fine initial burst of fast medium bowling. Our *Shankar's Weekly* came out with a doggerel. I remember a stanza or two, nothing which rhymed, seldom passed my memory bank unnoticed:

> Three cheers went up as Headley came in
>
> And the sahibs of Delhi made a great din
>
> but Headley was bowled and returned with a grin
>
> Sighing De Mello, DeMello.

De Mello, high up in cricket circles, was the refrain of the poem. Tarapore just got seven overs to bowl. What a waste. He was barracked while fielding on the boundary. Why were such gestures made? Rajinder Goel and Padmakar Shivalkar, both outstanding left arm spinners never played for India because of the presence of Bishan Singh Bedi. Tarapore couldn't play more than one because of Mankad.

In an unofficial Test against a Commonwealth XI, Umrigar raced from 90 to a century with two successive sixes, a harbinger of the Viru Sehwag days. His records speak for themselves. He hit 130 against England, in the first Test match India ever won at Madras in 1952. He was the first Indian to score a double century (223) at Hyderabad against New Zealand in 1955. He was the first Indian to cross 3,000 Test runs. He scored 560 runs against the West Indies in the 1953 series with two centuries. Till then only Modi had hit over 500 runs in a series, in 1948-49 home series against the Windies.

He had two bad tours of England, admitted. In 1952 he hardly got into double digits in the Tests, though he scored over 1,600 runs, including three double centuries on the tour. It happens in sport, Trueman became his bugbear. It was like Neil Harvey slaughtering Subhash Gupte in the Tests in India. Or Bedser getting the wicket of Arthur Morris 17 times. Umrigar did better in the next tour of 1959. After getting 29 and 39 at Headingly, he redeemed himself with a century (118) at Manchester, where Abbas Ali Baig, fresh from Oxford also hit a hundred. It was a sunny day. In the earlier tour Indians had batted twice after thunder showers.

For over a decade Umrigar and Manjrekar were the mainstay of our batting. Others like Hanumant Singh and Ghorpade came and went. Jaisimha had style and some fine scores to back him, but did not last that long. Manjrekar had thundering drives off the back foot and a pull to leg, but I found him uninspiring, despite his massive century in Delhi which I watched. He was slow, an ordinary fielder. He had a tally of seven centuries to Umrigar's 11, his average 39 to Umrigar's 42. Umrigar could be both cart horse and race horse. He could wheel his arm over after over. At the Kanpur Test in 1959 when Jasu Patel wreaked havoc against Australia (he took 9 wickets in the first innings), in the second innings Umrigar got four wickets for 27 runs in 25 overs from the other end. The cart-horse simile comes to mind when one thinks of the Test match at Bahawalpur, Pakistan in 1955 where he bowled 58 overs, gave away just 74 runs and took six wickets. Because of the paucity of speed merchants, he often opened the bowling. He bowled a bouncer (those days we used to call them 'bumpers') at Hanif Mohammad! Ramakant Desai, five foot something, was pitching short at Hanif from the other end.

Fans are odd birds, you never know what catches their fancy. When Sachin Tendulkar and Rahul Dravid were scoring heavily, VVS Laksman was my favourite, he of the imperturbable temperament and steely wrists. He cajoled the ball to the boundary, seldom hit it. Today Cheteshwar Pujara from the land of Ranji and Duleep, is nearest to the heart, not Virat Kohli. Umrigar was a favourite because of many reasons, our batting mainstay for a decade, our champion centurion in our first ever Test victory, saviour with another century against Pakistan after the debacle on a coir matting wicket in Lucknow in 1952 to help us win the series. And his bowling at Kanpur along with Patel against the Aussies.

He was made captain but soon fell out with the Board President, Ratibhai Patel over team selection. The president wanted Jasu Patel, Umrigar wanted a batsman, Hardikar. Patel threw his weight behind Jasu. Hardikar had missed his flight. Ghulam Ahmad had retired four days before the Test in Madras. Umrigar resigned. While there was some reason behind the Board president backing Jasu, officials have no business to interfere and meddle with selections. Umrigar is reported to have said, "I play for the country not for the selectors." Next day half an hour before the match, Mankad was taken for a chat near the toilets, (you can't beat that, can you?) and offered the captainship. Vinoo made it clear that he would select the team and he too dropped Jasu!

Umrigar scores 16,000 runs in first class cricket. He scored heavily in Ranji Trophy and won laurels as a bowler in the Duleep Trophy, though he played just a few. His stature as a big scorer and a gentleman was unique.

Keki on Keki:

As an outswing bowler and dependable batsman, Keki captained Govt. College Ludhiana and later UP Civil Services XI's. During lunch and tea intervals he wrote 12 volumes of poetry, and three acclaimed novels. During drink intervals he worked as Chairman (JIC) and Secretary Cabinet Secretariat. When too

Keki Daruwalla in action (Photo courtesy Keki Daruwalla)

old for cricket he worked as Member National Commission for Minorities, (2011-2014.) Distant relation of Jamshed Morenas, who went on the first two Indian cricket tours of England, 1886 and 1888 with the Parsis, and was coached by Lala Amarnath at Chail in 1956.

CHAPTER 2
Chandu Borde

by Fredun E. De Vitre

Over the years, I have been privileged to see, and for some years, to get to know at close quarters, several great Indian cricketers. These included the outstanding stalwarts from my community – the Parsees – who have made one feel proud with their achievements.

Polly Umrigar, a more-than-useful allrounder, a powerful hitter, a partnership-breaking off-spinner and a safe catcher, who I never saw in action but who I got to know many years later, as a genuine do-gooder, who revelled in helping others.

Nari Contractor, whose one performance is etched in memory: his commanding presence directing operations as captain of Gujarat against Bombay in a Ranji Trophy match at the Brabourne Stadium after his multiple surgeries and his remarkable return to the crease, having recovered from a near-death experience and who later became a 'sagaa' when his sister married a cousin (all Parsees, I suspect, are related in some way through a network of aunts and uncles and in-laws!); he seemed very stern and intense on the field, but was a bundle of fun and raucous laughter off it.

Rusi Surti, the tireless worker, bowling, batting, fielding, always wanting to be in the thick of the action, even if it

Chandu Borde (Pratyush Khaitan Collection)

meant taking on the likes of the dour Bill Lawry (he once flustered him with a "your father what goes?" sledge - a literal translation of the typical Parsee abuse, '*Taara Baap nu sujaych*' (one of the milder, cleaner ones); he later sought legal consultations and appeared to be a fighter, not willing to yield an inch.

And of course, Farokh Engineer, flamboyant, feisty, fearless -- you had to be exceptionally brave to pull off the feat of scoring 94 runs before lunch on the opening day of a Test match against Hall, Griffith, Sobers and Gibbs, as he memorably did in Madras in the 1967 Test; he too later became a friend and comes across as a trusting person, whose naïveté in some matters and plain speaking (when diplomacy is the order of the day) in others often contrasts with the sharp cricketing sense he displayed on the field; his sense of fun, though, has rarely left him.

But this piece is not about the Parsees and cricket. It is about My Favourite Cricketer. And though à la an Awards Nite, they would certainly be "nominees" for MFC and I enjoyed the performances of every one of the four mentioned above on the field of play and their company off it, none was "My Favourite Cricketer".

Why, then, this ramble about them? Simply because the one who was – and remains – my favourite cricketer was associated in some way with each of the above stalwarts.

MFC paired up with Umrigar in a 150-plus runs stand at Chepauk against Pakistan in 1961, remaining unbeaten on 177. MFC played his best all round cricket under the captaincy of Contractor, especially against Hanif Mohammad's Pakistan and against Ted Dexter's MCC side (as England on tour were then officially labelled) in the early 1960s, flowering as an all-rounder of exceptional ability. In the same innings at Chepauk in which Engineer got his 'almost-hundred' before lunch in 1967, MFC scored 125 against the blistering pace of Hall and Griffith and the wiles of Sobers and Gibbs--the FME century is remembered to this day, MFC's ton remains relatively unsung. He played his last Test, against the Australians in November 1969 at Bombay's famed Brabourne Stadium, which was also the last of Surti's Test career.

No, he is not a Parsee, though he could have passed off as one, with his dash and polished style in all he did. He is a proud Maharashtrian Christian, an odd admixture that made him an adventurous warrior with the disciplined work-ethic of a regular churchman.

My first sight of him was when as a 12-year old, I was allowed to go to the Brabourne Stadium on all five days of the October 1964 Test match against Australia–it was Dusshera and probably school vacation time. A very clear memory is of Chandu Borde calmly steering India to a historic victory on the last day. I was seated in the East Stand, the cheapest, with a 'season ticket' (i.e. a ticket for all five days) costing no more than Rupees five or thereabouts.

Between bouts of horror, seeing helpless ice cream and other vendors forced to lie prone and then being actually passed on down the rows, row by row, starting from the top (the vendor, not his wares - an abiding memory still), I glowed with pride at the sight of this tall, dashing gentleman walking out to bat at a critical juncture on that last day: his stride spoke of confidence, not arrogance as he calmly took matters into his own hands.

India tottered at 215 for 7, chasing 254, having lost Manjrekar earlier and Pataudi just then, after a long partnership. At the time, I remember feeling a sense of disappointment that my favourite cricketer Borde was relegated to number nine in the batting order, a decision made necessary as Nadkarni (unsuccessfully) and Surti (partially successfully) had been sent in as night watchmen to stem the fall of early wickets. It was a dream finish for Borde, and for the crowd, amongst whom was one specially enthused youngster whose own dream of seeing his favourite cricketer in action had been more than fulfilled. Two particular memories of that Test linger: of the crisp back-to-back boundaries his favourite cricketer hit, the latter, the winning stroke, a searing on-drive. And his catch to get rid of the dangerous-looking Vievers: unable to access full contemporary accounts of that match, memory seems to recall it was a brilliant effort at short cover, but perhaps that's more fantasy than fact.

Why Borde, you might ask. Why not, is my response? True, I have admired other more gifted players: Salim Durani, with filmy flair, and Borde's spin and late middle-order batting partner in the early sixties; Sunil Gavaskar, master technician, the epitome of concentration and discipline; Kapil Dev, with more natural talent than almost any other cricketer who ever played for this country, save perhaps Durani; Virender Sehwag, an incredible natural stroke-maker who was impossible to bowl to on his day. And yet, it is the relatively unsung Borde who was – and remains – my favourite cricketer.

Much of this had to do with his phenomenal exploits in the 1961-62 series against the MCC team led by Ted Dexter. For the television generation, it is difficult to imagine that at that time, one could know sportspersons only through radio commentaries and what was written about them and seen in still photographs as also occasionally, for a few fleeting moments, in a Films Division newsreel. Against Dexter's team, for the first time, India won a Test series (2-0) against England and the undoubted hero was Borde. It may well be that Vijay Manjrekar scored more runs and Durani took more wickets in that series, but somehow, to an impressionable nine-year cricket-mad brain, neither had the romanticism of Borde's all-round match-winning performances at Calcutta and Madras.

Consider his figures: 5 Tests: 3 scores of 50 and above, including in each innings of the Calcutta Test, the second innings 61 leading India to a win; 16 wickets, all of top-order batsmen of the calibre of Geoff Pullar, Peter Richardson, Bob Barber and the most majestic of them all, Dexter. Also, accounts of his electrifying fielding: the runs he saved patrolling the covers like a Panther (the moniker by which he came to be known as a result of his superlative fielding), the clean pick-ups and the accurate bullet-like throws. He and Durani made a handsome pair, sharing some great partnerships and complimenting each other's bowling skills.

Those were the days when Borde bowled his leg spin with considerable guile and dexterity: if memory serves me right, he had a slightly bent-low body action with what looked like a mis-step in the final delivery stride; he was fastish with no great flight and had a deceptive googly; in the Bombay Test of that series, he had Pullar stumped and Richardson bowled with a googly; in the Calcutta Test, he 'yorked' Dexter.

In his early years, he contended with the incomparable, but by then waning, Subhash Gupte and his brother Baloo and also V.V. Kumar from Madras. But he made his place in the team secure after his stand-out performances in that series against the MCC. And that is when he became the favourite of a little nine-year old fan who religiously cut out every photo of Chandu Borde (and thanks to *Sport & Pastime* weekly, there were an abundance of those) and pasted them in his scrap books (which are still available for viewing, and in 'mint' condition).

In fact, for decades more, that young nine-year old (who later engaged in activities like commentary and journalism that brought him to the periphery of the cricket world and still later in lawyering), had on his desk a faded press photograph of his favourite cricketer stuck on to a small red hard plastic Bayko-set cantilevered roof used as a stand, showing Borde playing a rasping square drive, superbly balanced on his back foot. In the course of changing work places, that photograph lost its place on the desk, but it is still lying somewhere, only waiting to be retrieved and restored to its right place on the desk, since the 'fandom' of that nine-year has never waned.

The record books state that Borde had cemented his place in the Indian team earlier, in 1958-59 against the West Indian tourists under Gerry Alexander. Dropped after a failure in the first Test, Borde was reinstated at Madras, as his replacement, R.B. Kenny, too failed. Another failure in the first innings spelt renewed danger to his place in the side. That's when his temperament came to the fore:

a 56 in the second knock – what he later described as a career-changing innings – sealed his place for the next two Tests. And in the last Test at Delhi, he created history: 109 in trying circumstances in the first innings and then, on the last day, staving off what at one stage seemed near-certain defeat, he reached 96 before disturbing a bail in the process of getting a hooked four off Roy Gilchrist in the last over of the match, four runs that would have brought up his second hundred.

Try as hard as I might, I have no recollection whatever of that series. The ironies of fate then took a hand: he fractured his thumb in the very first Test on the tour of England that followed and was out of the action at his peak. He returned to score a valiant 75 in the fourth Test at Old Trafford and did enough for Wisden to hail him as the outstanding success of an otherwise dismal tour.

Expectations were high when, after the dream series against the MCC, India embarked on a tour to the Windies in 1962, but it turned out to be a generally lack-lustre trip, highlighted by the gloom caused by the near-fatal injury to captain Contractor in the Barbados game. Borde excelled in one Test, getting a superb stroke-filled 93 on probably the world's quickest wicket at Sabina Park. It was obvious that the one quality of which there was no lack was sheer bravery in the face of pace like fire, without any protective gear that is today common-place. A younger, later generation may relate to him more if told that he was the 'Mohinder Amarnath of his time' in terms of his fearlessness.

Then followed a golden period: against Australia 1964 led by Bobby Simpson, against Mike Smith's MCC visitors and John Reid's New Zealanders, both in 1965. The Madras Test against the MCC is remembered for Nadkarni's spell of 21 consecutive maiden overs; largely forgotten is Borde's

5-for in that same Test. During the Kiwi tour, he stopped bowling because of a shoulder injury.

But he was worth his weight in the team for his batting alone and of course his fielding. He became one of the mainstays of the Indian batting. An innings-builder, a stylist in the mould of Vijay Hazare, his acknowledged mentor, technically sound but not obsessive about it. He had strokes all round the wicket, with the square cut and square drive being his most prolific scoring shots.

In March 1967, his status as India's best batsman was recognised when he was the only Indian chosen for the World XI against Barbados at Bridgetown for a commemorative game.

In many ways, Borde was the natural choice to take over from Contractor, but fate conspired to cut short Contractor's captaincy reign, pitchforking a young Nawab, who many felt was not quite then ready, into the captain's seat. The Nawab proved all the sceptics wrong, displayed great captaincy skills and made the India captaincy his own for the next decade. Borde, ever the team-man, sportingly played second-fiddle. I still recall the mixed feelings when news came through that he would captain India at Adelaide in Australia on the 1967-68 tour: disappointment at India being without Pataudi due to injury – but sheer, overwhelming delight that Borde was at last captain of India, even if only for one Test match.

His batting against the West Indian pacers Hall and Griffith on their 1966-67 tour of India was outstanding. Two centuries in three Tests. But the tours to England in 1967 and later that year to Australia were major set-backs: Borde just could not get going in any major way on both tours. He was expected to be the backbone of the batting, in tandem with his skipper Pataudi. The latter shone brightly, his deputy faltered badly.

Each time Borde was dismissed for a low score, one felt a sharp pain of sadness. Series averages of 10 and 20 did no justice at all to his huge talent (and majorly brought down his career average, which till then had hovered respectably around the late 40s). One said fervent prayers that his next outing would be a century, but apparently, the gods above had other ideas. They finally seemed to have heard the now 15 year-old's prayers only when the team left Australian shores and took on the Kiwis in a four-Test series on the return trip. India won its first series abroad and Borde was once more in the runs, topping the batting lists. The rhythm seemed back – and so were the smiles on that young 15-year old fan's face.

When the New Zealanders landed in India in 1969 for the return series, one had a palpable sense of anticipation that Borde would carry on with his heroics where he had left off and demolish the Kiwi attack. Alas, disappointment. Inducting youngsters into the Indian team became selectorial policy. Chetan Chauhan, Ashok Mankad, Ashok Gandotra, Ambar Roy and Eknath Solkar, all in. Chandu Borde, out. At least one forlorn youth, now seventeen years old, felt a sense of great betrayal and resentment against the selection committee. Emotion said my favourite Borde was being treated unfairly but logic admitted the need to induct young blood into the side.

In October that year, before the third Test at Hyderabad, these youngsters, including a callow youth from Bangalore going by the name of G.R. Viswanath, were put into Borde's charge as captain for the Board President's XI game at Indore, where the two got 63 and 68 and engaged in a 99-run partnership, during which the newcomer hopefully learnt some of the older pro's skills and the battle-scarred veteran got a close up view of the competition, and no doubt liked what he saw.

Then came Bill Lawry's Australians. Another fluent knock, this time an unbeaten century (113) for West Zone against the visitors at his home town Pune meant that he could not be overlooked for the first Test at the Brabourne. The excitement and exhilaration was back: Borde's return would assure stability in the middle-order. Prayer time once more: God, please let him score a century. But what can even God do when the likes of McKenzie and Gleeson are in full flow, bent on showing up slightly ageing reflexes? And so, once more, delight turned to disappointment. Scores of 2 and 18 meant Borde could be discarded without much fuss. A century on debut in the next Test at Kanpur by Viswanath, his replacement, ensured that his absence from the Test team became permanent.

A palpable pall of gloom descended on the young fan. That December, the youth even travelled to Madras for the last Test of the series, somehow managing a cheap-stand ticket, in the hope against hope that by some selection miracle, his favourite would be afforded one last chance to make a comeback, as he had done all those many years ago against the West Indies in his debut series at the same venue. Nada. India lost, after having Australia on the ropes at 24 for 6 in the second essay.

A chapter in the life of that young man came to an end with Borde leaving the Test scene. A batting average of about 36, after 55 Tests, somehow does not reflect his great contributions on the field at crucial moments. Till Kapil Dev and Ravi Shastri joined (and then surpassed) him, he remained the only Indian to get 3000 Test runs and 50 wickets.

But that young man's dream of meeting the champion had not yet been realised. That finally came about in April 1971 at the Ranji Trophy final, Bombay versus Maharashtra at the Brabourne. Borde captained Maharashtra, wily as ever, totally in command, brilliant field placements. Bombay, even without its four stalwarts who were touring the West Indies, proved too strong. Borde's handling of the left-arm spinner Vithal Joshi was an object lesson for young captains. Joshi's stock ball seemed to be the Chinaman, off-spin to the right-handers. He got 45 wickets for Maharashtra that season.The last two days of that match was that young lad's first commentary assignment for All India Radio (the first three days unfortunately coincided with an Inter-Arts exam, which parental diktat compelled the young lad to sit for, overruling his preference for doing the match commentary instead). Post-match, not yet 18, he nervously ventured down to the area where the trophies were being presented––and wonder of wonders, managed a shake-hand with the great man himself.

In later years, especially during the 1983-84 West Indies tour of India, the two crossed paths frequently, Borde as the Chairman of the Selectors now, and that young fellow, now slightly older, doing television commentary for four of the six Tests of that fascinating series. There were times when it was difficult to believe that I was actually conversing on cricket with my childhood hero. He has always been articulate, balanced, knowledgeable, most times understated, not one to ruffle feathers but with an ability to convince others of his point of view.

In one sense – not the pejorative one – he has been an 'establishment man', who went on to serve Indian cricket for many decades after that last Test in 1969. Selector of the junior and senior national teams, Chairman of the Selection Committee, manager and coach, most notably on the 1989 Pakistan tour when Tendulkar debuted and the 2007 tour of England, when his great experience and handling of the 'boys' under Dravid, after the disruptive Greg Chappell years, resulted in a series win for India.

In his understated, non-obtrusive way, he did not seek the limelight, but even the shadows cannot hide the lustre he brought to Indian cricket.

Fredun on Fredun:

Don't be fooled by the name: he's no Frenchman, despite the pretentious spelling of his last name. The first name, however, is a dead give-away: he's a true blue Bombaya 'bawaji', his only redeeming feature being his life-long passion for cricket.

Fredun E. De Vitre (Photo courtesy Fredun E. De Vitre)

For some years, he even inflicted his views on unsuspecting Doordarshan viewers with his commentaries. His cricketing abilities are just short of abysmal, although he claims to have been awarded the 'Man of the Match' and 'Best Bowler' trophies in the M. C. Chagla Memorial matches played annually between Judges and Senior lawyers, an unverified boast that is likely to be true and in any case is hilarious enough to be included in the book that he edited many moons ago, "Willow Tales – The Lighter Side of Indian Cricket." He echoes C.E. Montague's lament to Neville Cardus, voiced many years ago: "I love this game, truly love it, but I'll be damned if I can play it".

CHAPTER 3

Eknath Solkar

by Gulu Ezekiel

As with millions of schoolboys of that era, 1971 was the year that turned me into a cricket fan. On the cusp of my teen years, the victories in West Indies and England were gob-smacking enough to kick-start my love affair with the game.

The late GS Ramchand once angrily remarked: "Indian cricket did not start from 1971." Having captained India to their first win against Richie Benaud's Australians at home in 1959, Ramchand may perhaps have had reasons to be miffed that it was the team of '71 that had grabbed all the glory.

But then winning abroad was an alien concept for Indian cricket, having achieved the feat just once against lowly New Zealand in 1968. The mere thought of beating West Indies and England on their own soil was like dreaming the impossible dream.

There was a virtual smorgasbord of heroes for us to choose from that year. The veteran Dilip Sardesai whose double century in the first Test at Kingston helped the Indians to believe they had it in them after forcing West Indies to follow on; the legendary spin quartet of Bedi, Chandrasekhar, Prasanna and Venkataraghavan who proved that spin could win Test matches abroad; the dashing left-handed skipper Ajit Wadekar. And of course the mighty Sunil Gavaskar who showed the world that Indians did not flinch from the fastest bowlers even when opening the batting.

Eknath Solkar (Pratyush Khaitan Collection)

Like any young fan, I had my favourites. Syed Abid Ali was a doughty fighter, Farokh Engineer a flamboyant batsman/wicket-keeper and a 'Brylcreem Boy' to boot.

But it was a cricketer who seemingly played a bit-part in that heroic summer who captured my imagination. Eknath Solkar was half-jokingly described as the 'Poor Man's Sobers'--but then so was pretty much every player of that era who like the peerless West Indian did everything left-handed.

Just as Kapil Dev on Test debut in 1978 gladdened our hearts when he forced Pakistani opener Sadiq Mohammad to call for a helmet—who said Indians can't bounce?; just as Gavaskar proved Indians did not back off from pace like fire, so Solkar was in his own low-key way a pioneer in Indian cricket.

Not only did he dispel the popular perception that Indians cricketers were born with butter fingers, his unflinching courage at forward short leg—like Gavaskar while batting, unprotected—opened our eyes to the importance of sharp fielding.

Indian teams over the years have never been renowned for their fielding skills. But the team of the 70s barely let anything through their grasp.

At slip was Wadekar and Venkat, behind the wickets was Engineer and in the 'leg trap' Solkar and Abid Ali were ready to pounce on the half-chance as rival batsmen helplessly poked and prodded at a bewildering array of spin bowling.

It was like a spider's web wrapped round the batsman, ensnaring and suffocating him in their grip.

The English batsmen who were battered and bruised by Lillee and Thomson in 1974-75 may still be having nightmares and the scars from that traumatic tour. But no less traumatic was their tour of India in 1972-73 with huge crowds joining their fielders in appeal every time an England batsman got a nick (or did not).

Solkar hovering like a hawk just feet from the bat had a mesmeric effect on the batsmen as he snapped up a record 12 catches in the five Test matches.

The West Indians may not have been at their strongest in 1971. But they still had legends like Garry Sobers, Clive Lloyd and Rohan Kanhai in their ranks. In the first three of the five Tests, Solkar scored 50s batting low down in the order, propping up an extraordinarily long 'tail'.

India had never beaten West Indies in a Test match either at home or abroad since their first series in India in 1948-49. The victory in the second Test at Port of Spain had many standout performers. One world record (since broken) though was equaled in the Test and that was by Solkar with his six catches. That plus 55 in the first innings.

Indian cricket fans of my generation can never tire of watching two matches which are shown over and over again on our sports channels, the 1971 Oval Test and the 1983 Prudential World Cup final against West Indies.

One of the memorable images of the Oval Test is Solkar flat on the ground, clutching the ball as if for dear life, Gavaskar with both feet off the ground at slip and a stunned expression, Engineer mouth agape and bowler Venkat standing with arms held aloft and head thrown back in amazement at the wondrous catch.

Solkar has just caught Alan Knott for 1 in England's second innings and the removal of India's bogey man in the series opened the floodgates for India.

Part of Solkar's charm lay in his humble roots and his rustic English which would force England's batsmen to turn round to Engineer for 'translations' as he tried to sledge them from his vantage point. His fashionably long hair only added to his cult image for us youngsters.

A frustrated Sobers once passed a snide comment at him as he repeatedly played and missed. Solkar snapped back: "You play your way, let me play my way."

Back in India we could barely suppress shock at this kid's chutzpah. Our cricketers were not known to stand up to legends.

Time and again over the decades India's match winning spin bowlers have paid tribute to Solkar's catching skills which sharpened the edge of the bowling attack. Their predecessors had suffered terribly at the hands of sloppy fielders.

Like Sobers, Solkar too bowled a mixture of 'pace' and spin and though his Test bowling record is extremely modest, he had a few notable scalps including England's opener Brian Luckhurst who fell to his bowling three times in six innings in 1971. With three wickets in England's first innings in that memorable Oval Test, he was his side's most successful bowler till Chandra scythed through their second innings with six wickets.

In 1974 Solkar's innocuous dibbly dobblers tormented the formidable Geoffrey Boycott who succumbed to the left hander's gentle swing four times in six innings on that traumatic tour of England and may have been a factor in England's leading batsman going into self-exile for three years at the end of the first Test at Old Trafford.

Even as the batting crumbled to a miserable 42 all out in the second Test at Lord's, Solkar stood defiant with an unbeaten 18. It included a hooked six off India's nemesis, Chris Old.

His career was sandwiched between two Indian all-rounders of similar skills and abilities, Rusi Surti and Karsan Ghavri, both left handers. Ghavri was the best bowler of the trio by far, Surti marginally the best batsman and Solkar the best catcher. But Solkar achieved something the other two failed to do, a solitary Test century. That came in his home town of Mumbai at the Wankhede Stadium's first Test match against West Indies in 1975, a laborious effort that could not prevent the visitors winning the Test and a gripping series 3-2.

His final Test against England at Kolkata in 1977 was the second I saw from the stands. But for some years he continued to serve Mumbai in the Ranji Trophy as a winning captain. My one and only meeting with my hero was a very brief one during a cricket function in Mumbai in 1998. I was working for a private news channel at the time and had arranged for our Mumbai correspondent to interview him for the breakfast show where I was the sports anchor. Before the function I arranged for a video tape to be made of the interview and handed it over to him. All I got was a brief handshake and a nod. But that was enough for me.

A shadow spread across Indian cricket with Ekki's death in 2005 at the age of 57. Fifty-three catches in 27 Tests. Need one say more?

(A version of this article originally appeared in *The Cricketer* monthly dated August 2013. Reprinted with kind permission).

Gulu on Gulu:

Got his love for sports from his father and love of writing from his mother. First got hooked watching the 1966 FIFA World Cup on TV not far from Wembley. But it was in the historic Summer of '71 that the cricket obsession began.

Gulu Ezekiel

When flopped as a cricketer in school, turned to umpiring. When got fed up of standing for hours, turned to journalism. When after 20 years in print, radio, TV and Net, quit the rat race and turned freelance. With a dozen (or more) books to credit, this being the first ebook and first as editor.

CHAPTER 4

Sunil Gavaskar

by Hemant Kenkre

While growing up in the middle class area of Tardeo, Bombay (Mumbai), the place which I loved visiting was situated about a kilometer from where I lived. As a baby, my mother (a medical doctor) used to drop me off into the loving care of my Mami (maternal aunt) Mrs. Minal Gavaskar who lived on the top floor of Bhagirathi Bai building, a quaint block of four two-storied houses in the middle of which was an open area paved with compacted mud.

The visits to Mama (maternal uncle) Manohar Gavaskar, my mother's elder brother and Mami became a welcome haven for a boy growing up alone as the Mater went to her dispensary to practice medicine. Apart from delicious food and Marathi sugam-sangeet (light classical) songs sung by my affectionate aunt, the highlight of the trips was browsing through a brown, glass covered, wooden cabinet full of magazines.

The cupboard had a trove of them, majority of which were collected by my eldest cousin and the subject of this essay, my hero---Sunil Manohar Gavaskar. Needless to say, Dada as I have always called him showed a distinct preference for sports periodicals. Those acquainted me with names from Bradman and Merchant to Sobers, Kanhai and many more cavalier cricketers. Listening to stories recounted by my Mama, and his cousins who resided there, weaned me on their (and my) favourite game, cricket.

Hemant Kenkre (left, glasses) with Sunil Gavaskar to his left, Polly Umrigar (sitting, right), Dilip Sardesai (back row, right) and other Mumbai cricket stalwarts. (Photo courtesy Hemant Kenkre)

Dada was essentially my hero simply because he played cricket and everyone called him a prodigy. To watch him leave for a match with a small kit-bag and a bat in hand or see him standing in the veranda taking the muddy dirt out of his spiked shoes was aspirational for me, whose ambitions were to be like him. And, when my father used to show me his picture (usually with a raised bat) in the morning's newspaper, the sense of pride just kept swelling.

As time went by, the columns on his exploits started to get bigger and the frequency of his picture appearing in major newspapers began to increase. When Mama's family moved to distant Dadar, my loyalties shifted from Tardeo to 40-A Sir Bhalchandra Road, Dadar east. Just like I used to do at Tardeo, a key task he always gave me was to bowl throwdowns with a 'season' ball. Something I absolutely enjoyed in spite of ending with a sore shoulder after each half-hour session.

Earlier my throwdowns were done while standing on the steps of the passage outside his old flat. At Dadar they were effected while at the end of a special mat placed indoors in a long passage that separated the living room from his parent's and siblings' bed rooms. At both venues, the ragged orb of leather always came straight back, saving me the inconvenience of fetching the ball from distant corners. No flicks, no cuts, only straight drives. Many years later, when people raved about that particular shot, a small part in me always felt proud to play an itsy-bitsy, teenie-weenie part.

I must be one of the fortunate few who were privileged to see Sunil from playing Sunday fest (tennis ball) cricket in his home compound to his exploits for the country with university, club and state cricket in-between. Milind Rege, his bestie and my cricketing mentor, always reminds us of the number of shots he used to play all around the wicket, an attribute he used sparingly while holding the flag for India. What separated Dada from his peers, in Milind's (who went on to lead Bombay and serve the city's cricket) opinion, was the burning ambition he had and his ability to focus completely on the present situation.

One got many occasions to listen to his peers, seniors and heroes speak about him. Not just about his cricket but the way he approached the game.

While working (as a public relations consultant) on the

India-England series of 1993, I was in august company of M. L. Jaisimha, who was the brand ambassador of the sponsor. Among many stories that Uncle Jai told while touring across the country, was the way Dada evolved during the famed 1971 tour of the West Indies.

His work ethic and attitude were described in detail by the stylist from Hyderabad who said he realised he was in the company of a future great the way he approached the last Test at Port of Spain in Trinidad.

"To bat with a painful tooth and ensure the Test was drawn was a super human effort," said Dada's childhood hero. For one who was in awe of him since childhood, it was an amazing feeling to stand amid the multitude that welcomed Ajit Wadekar's victorious team as they landed at Santa Cruz airport in the late hours of a hot April night in 1971. To watch Dada standing on the steps of the airplane ladder with a glittering trophy in hand was exhilarating. My 'that's my brother' cries were lost in the deafening din that would have drowned the blast of a jet plane.

From 1971 to date, I've had many encounters with Dada's fans, peers and seniors. While on a social tour with the Cricket Club of India (CCI) team to Australia in 1982, a pleasant surprise awaited me as the team checked-in for a flight to Adelaide at Melbourne airport. Putting his bags on the check-in counter was Sir Garfield Sobers, who was also on our flight. When introduced as Sunny's cousin by (late) Kiran Ashar, his Bombay teammate, Sir Garry asked me to sit next to him during the short journey. The next hour and a half was full of questions posed to one of cricket's greatest all-rounder.

Sir Garry enquired about the well being of many from the Indian team that had beaten his side on the historic tour with particular reference to Dada and Gundappa 'Vishy' Viswanath. The Indian team, at that time, was locked in a Test series against Keith Fletcher's English side and Vishy had scored his first Test double hundred at Madras (Chennai). The team had come back after a drawn series against Australia where Dada had a dismal average in the three Test matches.

The legendary all-rounder wanted to know how Dada was doing, saying: "He will leave behind what happened on the Australian tour and come back very strong." Finishing the series with 500 runs from six Tests was a great return to form for Dada who had worked very hard before the England team touched Indian shores, playing even Saturday afternoon practice matches and local tournaments for his club and employers. "His grammar is impeccable and it is just a matter of time for him to find his form and rhythm," Sir Garry had foretold.

As we said goodbye to the genial legend on reaching Adelaide, he asked me a question concerning Dada. "Why does he wear that (guard) on his arm," he queried (pointing to his own forearm) while referring to the arm-guard Dada had started wearing. "Tell him that he does not need it. He's too good to wear that (guard)." Once back from down under, I conveyed Sir Garry's message about the arm guard to Dada when we were driving back together after a match. "Oh, did he say that," replied Dada, adding: "It's ok for him to say that. He never even wore a thigh pad when he played against the fastest of bowlers."

A hero is one who inspires and, to me, Dada has been a constant inspiration, even after he hung up his boots. As a club cricketer who played at a decent level, I always looked at Dada as a role model when it came to playing the game in the spirit it is meant to be played. When I stopped playing serious cricket, I took to writing and commenting on the game literally following his footsteps. When I worked with top notch brands in the communications sphere, the discipline that Dada always showed while working rubbed off on me. Even when he was at the top of his game and career, Dada never missed a day in the office.

A lesser known attribute of Dada is his sense of loyalty and the camaraderie he still shares with his close friends. His son Rohan once told us a story how Dada refused to buy a brand as it competed with another one that he had endorsed more than two decades ago. Throughout his career, Dada stuck to his club Dadar Union (barring a few years as a playing member for the CCI, considered a prestige then) telling the management to call him whenever the club fell short of players till a few years after he had retired.

Each year, Dada hosts a party inviting a few close friends and many cricketers with whom he has shared a dressing room from his school days and onwards. The soiree attracts well known names from the world of cricket and a few 'A'- listers from the world of entertainment. More than his interactions with well known names, I always find his conversations with his old mates from Bhagirathi Bai Buildings very fascinating.

Huddled in a group, they discuss memories. With them, Dada goes back to becoming a schoolboy, once again, recollecting (among other things) the tennis ball matches that they had played in the era of the 60s. For that short moment of time, the legendary opener gets transported back in time while laughing, cracking jokes and leg pulling, exactly how it must have happened in the mud-paved compound of their old homes many decades ago.

Dada's legion of fans goes across continents. He singlehandedly changed the way Indian cricket, and cricketers were perceived not just on the field but off it too. He has had his detractors and has handled them in a way only he could, with a certain dignity and loads of class. As a die-hard fan, it feels great when people speak in glowing terms about your hero and his phenomenal exploits that raised the value of Indian cricket in foreign shores.

While on a music tour to the Caribbean in 1985, I had a delightful encounter with a band of cricket lovers in Trinidad. I kept badgering our host to take me to the Queen's Park Oval where India had established their first Test series victory against the West Indies. Driving me down to the Savannah, where the iconic cricket stadium was located, my host ushered me into the ground where my hero had made his Test debut as a 21-year old. As I soaked in the atmosphere imagining what must have taken place more than a decade and a half ago, we came across a long bar which overlooked the green expanse of the cricket field.

Sitting at the bar were an enthusiastic lot of members discussing cricket while sipping their poison to beat the afternoon heat. The hot topic of the day - Is Vivian Richards better than Rohan Kanhai? - was interrupted when my host introduced me, saying I was a cricketer from Bombay who was related to Sunil Gavaskar. To my amazement, the heated comparisons between the current and past West Indian masters ended abruptly. My new bar friends (one of them being former West Indies international Joey Carew) rose up in unison, put their glasses up in the air in salute, saying: "Cheers to the Maastah!"

Hemant on Hemant:

A certified cricket-o-file, Hemant Kenkre, a communications professional and cricket columnist, was initiated into the game by the legendary Vinoo Mankad. A former Bombay University opener and captain of the Cricket Club of India team, he was known to hold his own on the wet wicket (pun intended). The only thing that can take him away from cricket is music and, ever since he has started using headphones, life's been good.

CHAPTER 5

Salim Durani

by Amrit Mathur

As a child I watched Rajasthan play in the Ranji Trophy at different venues in Jaipur-Chowgan stadium, Maharaja College and Ganapati Nagar Railway ground. I remember watching my childhood heroes, all smartly dressed in silk shirts rolled up to the elbows, pleated flannels and polished white spikes.

The most strikingly handsome of them was Salim Durani, the Prince. As he walked out of the players' shamiana one admired his slow deliberate walk, his regal presence, his cool swagger .And you couldn't help noticing that his shirt collar was turned up. Total style!

Salim-bhai was part of a Rajasthan Ranji team that consisted of assorted princes, notably Hanumant Singh of Banswara and Rajsingh-ji from Dungarpur. Salim-bhai did not come from a similar privileged background but was cricket royalty who happened to be in the employ of Bhagwat Singh, the Maharana of Udaipur, President of the Rajasthan Cricket Association and captain of the Rajputana team.

Though a 'commoner', for common cricket fans Salim-bhai was the undisputed king. Ranji Trophy games those days attracted a handful of loyal spectators but the majority of those present turned up to pay homage to him. End of play these subjects would crowd round him with invitations of a night out on the town.

Salim-bhai was cricket's original popular star-- celebrated for his film star looks, his flair and flamboyance and the tantalising prospect he held out of creating magic when in the middle. In the 1960's he was cricket's Daredevil and khatron ka khiladi.

Salim Durani with Amrit Mathur (Photo courtesy Amrit Mathur)

Memory: Ranji Trophy final, Rajasthan versus Bombay. Venue: Railway stadium, Jaipur--located in the middle of a residential colony which had a matting wicket and short boundaries at square leg.

As happened so many times before, Bombay crushed Rajasthan with Vijay Manjrekar and Manohar Hardikar scoring big daddy hundreds. But my lasting memory is Salim-bhai hitting a Ramakant Desai bouncer for six - the ball sailed over square leg to land on the railway track, a monster hit!

After the game I stood in a queue to get my autograph book signed by him.

Memory: I was helping Tiger Pataudi choose his 'best ever' Indian team for some publication. Tiger, quite typically, was disinterested in the exercise but reluctantly named the players that selected themselves. Vijay Merchant, Sunil Gavaskar, Kapil Dev, Sachin Tendulkar, Anil Kumble, Vijay Hazare and the others.

Then he paused and thought hard, searching for the other names to complete the list .He weighed options, picked someone, then changed his mind. Vinoo Mankad or Bishan Bedi? Rahul Dravid or GR Viswanath? What about Subhash Gupte?

Confused, and bored, he decided to opt out. You put in anyone you want he told me, as long as you have Salim's name there.

Anyone who knew Tiger even remotely would confirm that was high praise. Tiger wasn't the type to get easily impressed.

Memory: Ranji Trophy game at the Sawai Man Singh stadium, Jaipur. Rajasthan is batting, I am sitting next to Salim-bhai in the dressing room (located at square leg) on those old fashioned moodas. Salim-bhai is padded up, in next, but calm - no sign of stress, anxiety, nerves.

A wicket falls, someone shouts to alert Salim-bhai who, hearing the commotion pulls himself together. But there is a minor problem: he can't find his bat! But no problem, really: he casually picks up a bat from a kitbag lying around and walks out.

In the middle he is in control — all style, elegance and class. Every ball middled—that too with someone else's bat!

Memory: Delhi playing Rajasthan at the Kotla in the 1974-75 season. Salim-bhai nearing the end of his career, Delhi on top.

Salim-bhai attempts to late cut Rakesh 'Pappuji' Shukla, misses and a young Delhi fielder at slip passes a rude remark. No reaction from the aging master.

An interesting passage of play followed thereafter. Every time Pappuji bowled, Salim-bhai would step leg-side to cut late, even balls pitched up or close to the stumps, forcing the slip fielder to go fetch the ball.

This went on for a while till Salim-bhai finally nicked one and was caught behind. Walking back, he stopped to have a polite word with the Delhi fielders around the bat. "*Thoda cricket hame bhi khelna aata hai*" ("Even I know how to play a little cricket") he said.

Memory: Salim-bhai the player was a big talent who, unfortunately seriously underperformed and did grave injustice to himself. Starting out as a wicket-keeper he turned into a quickish left arm spin bowling from a whippy action that produced sharp turn and disconcerting bounce.

His batting was classical, he judged length early, had time and was rarely rushed. Like Kapil Dev, his junior by a generation, Salim-bhai was good enough to play for India and bat in its top order.

Like Kapil, cricket came naturally to him, it was a gift. He made it look simple and easy — it was never a burden. Salim-bhai will always be remembered as a free spirited entertainer who gave joy, not just by producing sixes on demand, but for his effortless ease and basic excellence.

Like his cricket, there is much to like about Salim-bhai the person. He is extremely charming, courteous, polite, cultured in an old world manner-- a pleasant, likeable person with a huge talent for making the wrong choices, especially in financial matters.

For years even when at his peak, Salim-bhai lived on the edge in a manner of speaking. But such is the goodwill he enjoys, he always had someone ready to hold his hand and take him through.

Memory: A reception was organised for the visiting England team at the CCI, Mumbai. Past Indian cricketers too were present, and it was a wonderful cricket evening full of fun. Salim-bhai, inevitably, was in the middle of the loudest group holding court, entertaining everyone with cricket stories from his playing days.

That these stories can't be retold--owing to the sensational nature of their content--is another matter!

Memory: June 2018, Afghanistan's inaugural Test match versus India at Bengaluru.

Syed Saba Karim (then GM, BCCI) called to say they wanted Salim-bhai to be present in Bengaluru because of his Afghan connection, wanting me to get him to agree. When I reached out to him, Salim-bhai graciously agreed but pointed out he wasn't in the best of health.

Despite this, he made the trip from Rajkot and was at the Chinnaswamy Stadium (along with Col Rajyavardhan Singh Rathore, Minister of Sports) to shake hands with the two teams before the toss.

I am not sure what the Afghan team made of this, but the Indian team appreciated the gesture and looked at Salim-bhai, superstar of the past but now old and frail, with awe and admiration.

Amrit on Amrit:

A cricket person who joined the Indian Railway Service, but whose career suffered a series of friendly accidents. Life changed track and led to a fresh innings as an insider in sport administration. Especially with the BCCI where became manager of the Indian team/General Manager/Member, World Cup Committee. Had a longish stint with Delhi Daredevils in the IPL and interesting cameos with UP/ MP/ Railways / Rajasthan and Uttarakhand cricket associations. To round of the 360 degree sports loop worked as Secretary, SAI and also as Advisor, Ministry of Sports, Government of India. Though an insider, played a double role—as a columnist--looked at cricket from the outside. Writings provided perspective gained from the long years in sport. One of those who lucked out to witness important cricket events from the BCCI board room, the Indian team dressing room and the IPL dugout.

CHAPTER 6

Vijay Hazare

by Kersi Meher-Homji

In my 70 years of cricket watching at the highest level I have admired superlative batsmen -- Frank Worrell, Tom Graveney, Neil Harvey, Norm O'Neill, Garry Sobers, Hanif and MushtaqMohammad, Bert Sutcliffe, Graeme Pollock, Sunil Gavaskar, Vivian Richards, Doug Walters, Ian and Greg Chappell, Allan Border, Brian Lara, Sachin Tendulkar, Steve and Mark Waugh, Ricky Ponting, Rahul Dravid, VVS Laxman, Kumar Sangakkara, Michael Clarke, Virat Kohli … great batsmen all.

Still my hero number one is Vijay Hazare. Always was, always will be. Why? To me he was cricket personified; elegant and reliable.Also there is a personal reason.

The thrill of bicycling rather than a love of cricket prompted me, a 10 year-old village boy in Udvada (a village in Gujarat), to visit a stranger's house miles away to listen to my first cricket commentary.

My elder brother Vispy was keen to know the score of the Calcutta (now Kolkata) unofficial test between "Jock" Livingston's Commonwealth XI and India in 1949-50. However, in our tiny village, electricity was not available in day time. The only battery-operated radio was owned by a cricket fan in the next village.

That time I had no interest in cricket but the prospect of a long bicycle ride was exciting. When we reached the radio owner's house there were about 15 people listening to the commentary. They were silent as Vijay Hazare was on 97 then. Had he reached his century with a four or a few singles, my interest in cricket would have remained lukewarm.

Captain Vijay Hazare (seated centre) with the 1952 Indian team in England (Gulu Ezekiel Collection)

But Hazare took his time. It was gripping. My heart missed a beat several times as he defended stoutly. After 10 minutes he was still on 97. There was total silence apart from the commentators' voice. No one in the room dared to sneeze or cough, let alone speak!

Hazare was still on 97 after few more minutes as we were glued to our seats. Eventually he did reach his ton and then galloped to 175 not out against a strong attack which included George Tribe.And a cricket lover was born.

Hazare was an all-time Indian cricket great. A classy batsman with faultless technique, solid defence and elegant stroke-play, he was a man of few words who often was a crisis specialist, coming to India's rescue in her darkest hours.

India achieved their first Test win under Hazare's captaincy, against England at Chennai (then Madras) in 1952. Yet he was not an inspiring captain. Vijay Merchant, another prolific Indian batsman and a close friend, wrote in the foreword to Hazare's autobiography *Cricket Replayed* (1974): "I wish Hazare had never captained India. He was never a leader of men. He was always a disciplined soldier, never a commander."

Hazare was the first Indian to reach 1,000 and 2,000 runs in Test cricket, scoring 2,192 runs at 47.65 in 30 Tests, hitting seven centuries. His most prolific home series was against the West Indies in 1948-49, when he collected 543 runs at 67.87, including two centuries, in two Tests in Mumbai. His unbeaten 134 in the second Test saved India and his 122 in the drawn final match brought India close to its first Test win.

Some of Hazare's best innings were played when they were most needed. In the second innings of the Leeds Test of 1952, India had lost their first four wickets for no run, with England's raw fast bowler Fred Trueman and master seamer Alec Bedser threatening to rout the tourists for the lowest total in Test history. Hazare was on the massage table, nursing a painful injury. Gallantly he came out and blunted the attack with an innings of 56.

In the same series at The Oval, India were tottering at five wickets down for six runs with Trueman and Bedser on the rampage on a wet, treacherous pitch. Hazare scored 38 out of India's 98. "It was the innings of my life", he wrote.

However, his finest performance was in the Adelaide Test of 1947-48 against the Don Bradman-led team that would soon become known as the 'Invincibles'. India had lost the previous two of the three Tests by huge margins and appeared set for further humiliation after Australia amassed 674.

Hazare came to the middle with India 69 for 3 and facing oblivion. Undaunted, he scored 116. Forced to follow on, India was 2 down for naught when in came Hazare again, this time making 145. He became the first Indian to hit centuries in both innings of a Test, and that too against the fury of express bowlers Ray Lindwall and Keith Miller.

These centuries of guts and character moved Bradman to write: "Hazare gave a display which ranks with one of the finest seen in this country. There is no doubt Hazare was among the most accomplished batsmen ever to visit Australia and cricket-lovers are indebted to him for the enjoyment he gave them."

Although labelled a slow scorer and inelegant in England, Australian critics were full of praise for his stylish batting. R.S. Whitington commented: "The [Archie] Jackson-like grace of Hazare fired the imagination of the Australian public."

Noted commentator Bobby Talyarkhan described him as "immaculate in appearance and studied in every movement, Hazare might well be dubbed the Indian Jack Hobbs".

Hazare's on-drives were similar to Greg Chappell's. His hooks, cuts and cover-drives were equally awe-inspiring. In The Romance of Indian Cricket, Sujit Mukherjee wrote, "Should ever a sculpture be made of Hazare, it should be in this, the most glorious of his batting postures, in playing the cover-drive."

Only a change bowler, he twice bowled Bradman, once each in the Sydney and Adelaide Tests. When interviewed in 2000 he said, wiping away nostalgic tears, that it was this feat he remembered more than his centuries.

Hazare was coached in 1938 by the Australian leg-spinner Clarrie Grimmett. "I consider myself very lucky to receive coaching from Grimmett so early in my career," he told me in a letter. "Practicing with him every day improved my batting technique and gave me confidence."

After scoring twin hundreds in the January 1948 Adelaide Test, Hazare received a gold watch from the South Australian Cricket Association, and the Prime Minister Robert Menzies warmly congratulated him. But for him the greatest thrill was the praise he received from his mentor, 'Guru' Grimmett, who said, "Vijay, I am a very proud man today."

Hazare had fond memories of Australia. "I wish it was possible for me to revisit Australia where I had such a delightful time," he wrote to me in 1977. "I remember the Sydney Cricket Ground (SCG) because it was here that I scored my first century in Australia, against New South Wales. But for me the ground par excellence is the Adelaide Oval. It made a vivid spectacle with the St Peter's Cathedral bestowing blessings on me", reminisced Hazare, a Catholic.

If only Hazare had played for a stronger side. Time and again he rescued his country with a big score but before he could unstrap his pads in the pavilion a couple of wickets would topple, so brittle was India's batting.

At home Hazare was supreme. In a Ranji Trophy match for Baroda against Holkar in 1946-47, he added 577 runs with Gul Mahomed, a world record that stood till 2006.

In the epic Pentangular final for The Rest against The Hindus, a team including nine Test players, in Mumbai in 1943-44, he added 300 runs in 332 minutes for the sixth wicket with his younger brother Vivek. As Vivek held one end up with 21, Vijay attacked with gusto. He went from 294 to 300 with a six to become the first Indian to hit two triple centuries in first-class cricket. He went on to score 309 out of The Rest's total of 387 all out. This 79.8 per cent monopoly in scoring remained a world record in first-class cricket for many decades.

In a purple patch that summer, he scored 1,027 runs in six consecutive innings, (248, 59, 309, 101, 223 and 87). At first-class level from 1934 to 1966, he amassed 18,740 runs at 58.38, hitting 60 centuries (including eight double and two triple centuries, highest score being 316 not out). He also took 595 wickets at 24.61, best spell being 8 for 90.

When India's involvement in match-fixing was confirmed in 2000 it affected him greatly. His daughter-in-law said that he cried uncontrollably that day.

In the Bombay Test against England at Brabourne Stadium in December 1951, Hazare scored 155 run out. This was the first Test I had seen and was delighted to have witnessed magnificent centuries by Graveney, Pankaj Roy and Hazare.

Although we exchanged letters and I watched him score centuries against England and Pakistan in Bombay Tests, I did not have a chance to have a verbal chat with my hero.

The nearest I came to him face-to-face was in the late 1950s when he had retired from Test cricket. In a non-first-class match at Parsi Gymkhana in Bombay he scored a magnificent double century for Catholic Gymkhana. I approached him hesitatingly and he responded with a smile.

When Hazare was awarded Padma Shri in January 1960, I wrote a letter of congratulations to him. I was thrilled to receive his reply on February 16 that year highly appreciating my letter. Among other things he wrote, "The honour done to me is in fact honour done to the great game of cricket."

This was the first of 10 letters and numerous Christmas cards he lovingly sent to me in Mumbai and in Sydney. All his letters and Cards are preserved by me along with letters and cards I have received from Sir Donald Bradman, Vijay Merchant, Sunil Gavaskar, Bishan Bedi...

I posted to Hazare clippings of my cricket articles and books and he always had a word of praise which really inspired me to better efforts. One of his letters was very nostalgic: "I nostalgically remember Australia in general and Adelaide in particular. I am not likely to forget my moments of thrill of the company of my cricket guru Grimmett, the cultured Duleepsinhji and the connoisseur Menzies, then the PM of Australia… I still gratefully remember the gestures of Bradman and Miller writing flattering tributes in the souvenir of my Benefit match… Any news of my master Grimmett?"

Hazare was honoured in the season 2002-03 when a domestic limited-overs cricket competition was named after him, the Vijay Hazare Trophy.

When Vijay Samuel Hazare passed away in December 2004 aged 89, it was a personal loss to me.

The dynamic Australian all-rounder Keith Miller, who incidentally died two months before Hazare, had paid him the ultimate tribute in 1967. "Vijay Hazare, one of the most gentlemanly cricket giants of all time, has had his fair share of bumpers hurled at his head in his heyday. And how brilliantly and viciously he hammered this none-too-easy delivery to master. He was a cricketing giant by any yardstick."

Reading and rereading this tribute was the consolation I needed. Even now the memories of Hazare my hero linger.

Kersi on Kersi:

If you want to read on quirkiness in cricket, Kersi is your man. Author of Out for a Duck, Six Appeal and Cricket Quirky Cricket he has written many magazine articles on the game's oddities.

Although in his early 80s, he still plays social cricket matches, retiring hurt after scoring a few runs to improve on his batting average! But there is a serious side to Quirky Kersi.

Kersi in action (Photo courtesy Kersi Meher-Homj)

A retired research Virologist he has written 13 serious books on cricket including Nervous Nineties, Dramatic Debuts and Swan Songs, Cricket's Great All-Rounders, From Bradman to Kohli and the bestselling The Waugh Twins. His heroes are Vijay Hazare, humorous writer PG Wodehouse and musician Pankaj Mullick. Uncle KR Meher Homji kept wickets for India in one Test in England in 1936.

CHAPTER 7

GR Viswanath

by Suresh Menon

I was 12 when, during a Ranji Trophy match, I ran onto the field to shake hands with Gundappa Viswanath. "There are no cricketers," wrote English player and author Ian Peebles, "like those seen through 12-year-old eyes."

By then Vishy (familiarity breeds contraction), barely 24, was already one of Bengaluru's favourite icons – as dependable as the Vidhana Soudha, as approachable as Cubbon Park. When relatives asked me what I wanted to be when I grew up, I answered "Viswanath."

Sometimes we choose our heroes; at other times, proximity, convenience or back story mean they choose us. We choose them as much to glory in their successes as to empathise with their failures, and thereby to understand those two Kiplingesque imposters when they visit us. The rationalisation comes much later, of course.

I must have been eight when I first became aware of Viswanath and put him on a pedestal. Boys that age are flexible in picking heroes. Accomplished performers, fictional characters, comic book eccentrics, imaginary beings that exist only in their heads — they can all make the grade.

Perhaps you see a bit of yourself in your hero, perhaps you hope that there is a lot of your hero in you. Perhaps it doesn't really matter. If the game mirrors society as a whole, perhaps the individual player mirrors something uniquely personal.

Suresh Menon with GR Viswanath and Sunil Gavaskar
(Photo courtesy Suresh Menon)

The hero-as-role-model is not a concept many are comfortable with. Heroes are heroes and role models are role models, but occasionally they overlap, as they did with Vishy. It meant we did not have to readjust our sights as we grew older; few heroes are heroes forever and those of innocent boyhood often turn out to be disappointing in adulthood. Not Vishy.

By shaking hands with Vishy, I had been ushered into an exclusive club, and I began following him wherever he played — league matches, friendly tennis ball knockabouts, first class and international matches, the lot. The YMCA ground once witnessed a wonderful battle between Vishy's State Bank of India and Bhagwat Chandrasekhar's Syndicate Bank.

The grass was thick all around, and some of others' finest drives didn't make it to the boundary. Vishy driving Chandra was a treat — he seemed to have calculated the precise height he needed to drive at so the ball would just skim the tops of the clumps of grass. Vishy's technical mastery was enhanced by his innovative ability.

When he was making his classic 97 not out in Chennai, West Indies captain Clive Lloyd paid him the compliment of placing a man at cover-point for Andy Roberts, the world's fastest bowler then.

Vishy is the quintessential Indian batsman, all wristy grace and mischief, eastern magic and unattainability. Indians of his generation liked their sporting heroes to be modest, self-effacing men with a touch of nobility about them. In Viswanath, they found the mix that might make him seem today like a character out of fiction. It was a mature choice for an eight-year-old to make all those years ago. You came for the square-cut and stayed for the charm.

Occasionally sport throws up a performer who embodies its spirit and its link with the best in us, reminding us that there is more to it than winning and losing. It is a necessary counter to the partisanship and cynicism inherent in supporting a team.

Vishy was the equal of any batsman in the game, a modern-day Victor Trumper whose statistics didn't hint at the enormous joy he brought to spectators everywhere. An average of nearly 42 over 91 Tests suggests a commendable disdain for padding the figures with easy runs when there was no real challenge. India never lost a Test when Viswanath made a century, and he made 14 of them, beginning with his debut 137 against Australia in Kanpur in 1969-70, where, as a 20-year-old, he struck 25 boundaries. Trinidad, Melbourne, Lord's, Kolkata and Faisalabad all witnessed classic centuries.

But to discuss Viswanath in terms of runs and averages would be like reducing Michelangelo to the number of brush strokes or square inches per canvas. Vishy was the sportsman's sportsman, with character and temperament that brought lustre to the game, which, when he was batting or captaining, exhibited its best facet. He brought out the best behaviour in people too.

In an era when success is merely a set of figures properly arranged, and anything beyond that is seen as unnecessary, a hankering after aesthetic significance may sound strange. For sheer beauty we are yet to see anything to match a late cut or a leg glance or indeed the patented square cut by Viswanath. Often, this was beauty made thrilling by danger, of the prospect of dismissal. He often got his eye in by playing the kind of shots an average batsman never produces in a lifetime.

Sunil Gavaskar rated Viswanath higher than himself because he had more shots for every delivery. Ranji, the spiritual father of the wristy, stylish Indian batsman, batted as if he had "no bones" — a description that fit Viswanath nicely.

At 18, he was mature enough to score a double-century on first class debut for Karnataka against Andhra. It was a message for those in authority, who felt he was too small to play serious cricket.

"I didn't play state schools cricket at all," he once said, "I heard that I was kept out because I was too thin or too small or too ugly." That's a typical Viswanath reaction to disappointment: no malice, merely a shrug of his shoulders and self-deprecating humour.

In Mumbai in 1973, when he made his second Test century, England's Tony Greig picked him up in his arms and cradled him to the full-throated approval of a packed house. It was in Mumbai seven years later that Viswanath, now captain of India, recalled England's Bob Taylor after the umpire had given him out. It cost India the match, as Taylor and Ian Botham put on 171 runs, but it earned the team a reputation for playing to a higher set of rules than required by the scorebook. The Indian team was merely reflecting its captain's philosophy of fair-mindedness. How you played the game was important.

In the nearly four decades since Viswanath retired, other middle-order batsmen have made more runs for India, played more Tests, been part of more victories. But none have had his unique combination of heart and wrist. He didn't just patently enjoy his game, he communicated it to the spectators. "Vishy", they called him, like he was a dear friend. Which he remains, to everybody who saw him play.

Suresh on Suresh:

Went from being a promising cricketer to a has-been without a significant career in-between. The time saved he spent becoming in turn India's youngest sports editor and then editor of a national newspaper. He is also the first editor of Wisden India Almanack, and author of the books Bishan: Portrait of a Cricketer, Pataudi: Nawab of Cricket and Sachin: Genius Unplugged. When he turned 50, he was finally convinced he would never play for India.

CHAPTER 8

Kapil Dev

by Dr. Narottam Puri

It is a strange paradox that if one were asked to choose the best India XI or World XI, one is often stamped, at least I am, funding it difficult if not impossible to choose. But when it comes to choosing India's best all-rounder ever, my mind barely shows evidence of any dichotomy.

Having had the pleasure of watching the two greatest all-rounders of India play --Vinoo Mankad and Kapil Dev, I can say with confidence and reasoning why my mind ticks the box in front of the name Kapil Dev.

Vinoo was undoubtedly one of the greats of Indian cricket-- superb left-arm spin bowler, an opening batsman who had moved the needle quite a bit from amateur to professional in Indian cricket. He also captained India in six Tests. He was a safe fielder, superb to his own bowling and won India many a match, particularly on Indian pitches.

Despite his 2000-plus runs and 162 Test wickets, his world record (broken only after 52 years) first wicket partnership with Pankay Roy and his having a cricketing term ('Mankaded') coined for running a batsman out at the non-strikers end for backing up too for, I would, unhesitatingly opt for Kapil Dev as the best all− rounder India has ever produced and one of the all time greets the game of cricket has ever seen.

Dr. Narottam Puri with Kapil Dev (Photo courtesy Dr. Narottam Puri)

I can never forget that day the 11th of February 1981 at Melbourne, Australia in the 1980–81 series. India had been thrashed by the home team at Sydney in the first Test and had fought bravely to draw the second Test at Adelaide with the late Chetan Chauhan missing his century by three runs but Sandeep Patil scoring his first Test ton (174).

Melbourne was India's chance to level the series which India did thanks to the heroic spell by Kapil Dev (5 – 28) in the second innings. GR Viswanath's century had given India hope and Australia were to bat last on a pitch where the odd ball kept low.

On that Wednesday, the 11th February, Yashpal Sharma knocked on my room door at the Windsor, where we, the commentators were staying with the team. He asked me to accompany him to take a look at Kapil's injured leg due to which he had not been able to share the new ball with Karsan Ghavri on the 4th evening.

Kapil injury seemed bad and I told him it would be advisable for him not to take the field, given that he would be needed in the upcoming New Zealand tour (the team was to fly to New Zealand immediately after the Melbourne Test). But Kapil was adamant, telling me he will come what may.

He did, took 5 for 28 (Yardley, Border, Marsh, Lillee and Higgs)--India bowled Australia out for 83 and won the Test by 59 runs to level the series. Injuries never stopped him.

It is my good future that Kapil's debut tour to Pakistan in 1978 was my first visit to that (or any foreign country, for cricket) country.

India's celebrated spinners were put to the sword and India not only lost the three match series 0 – 2, the halo around the spinners faded and Bedi lost his captaincy. One man, though not exceptionally successful, drew attention and promised a bright future – the debutant Kapil Dev. When Sadiq Mohammad asked for the helmet against Kapil, the world knew that India had at last a fast bowler who could bowl 140 kmh. He was the quickest Indian fast bowler I had seen since Ramakant Desai in 1960– 61.

131 Tests, 225 ODIs --434 Test and 253 ODI wickets; 5,248 Test runs and 3,783 ODI runs are enough to stamp anyone as a magnificent cricketer.

Now add 74 ODI/s 34 Tests as captain with the 1983 World Cup triumph in England changing the face, belief and stock of not just the Indian cricket team but charging the very outlook of a nation. Now put in a dash of a brilliant fielder with a safe pair of hands – the ingredients mesh into India's best ever all-rounder – the one and only Kapil Dev, whose name shall forever remain in the list of all-time great all-rounder the world has ever seen.

Kapil's greatness lay in his simplicity – to life, to cricket, to the spirituality of trying to do one's best, fighting to the last. A naturally gifted athlete, he worked hard, not just on his fitness and technique but also on his self-development. He remained, till the end of his playing days, a complete team man.

One of the joys of my life has been the gift I've had of watching him play, commentate on radio or TV on his matches, shared many a moment outside the field with a delightful, simple soul. In fact, we once shared the mike in an ODI at Faridabad, after he retired.

Kapil Dev's lasting gift to Indian cricket will not be the many matches – Tests, ODIs, series or even the World Cup that India won but the fact that his exploits stirred the imaginations and fired the belief of legions of young Indians, who took up bowling fast and filling up the large void. His skills, his athleticism, his simple almost rustic but rugged appeal as a personality and his exploits made a nation start to believe in itself and the success that was always a dream become a reality. Kapil Dev made a nation believe.

Tomes have and can be written about Kapil but to me the best lines will remain the one I penned in the book his wife Romi brought out for him – "I never saw Kapil just in the Whites of cricket, it seems he was draped in the national tri-colour every time he stepped onto the field"--or words to this effect.

Thank you, KAPIL!

Doc on Doc:

It used to be said frustrated doctors who couldn't become surgeons became anaesthetists, possibly true of Dr. Puri— could not progress beyond university and club cricket, so became a commentator. Trying to row two boats simultaneously — practice of medicine and radio and TV sports and a bit of writing, did wonders— shamateur in most fields. Somehow lasted for more than four decades in sports coverage and still going in medicine. Obsessed with questioning, created and presented India's longest running TV quiz show—Sports Quiz which ran for 18 years (1974-92)—and spawned two best sellers, Cricket Quiz and Sports Quiz.

Sadly reduced to writing " Down memory lane " pieces for the likes of Gulu Ezekiel. Unable to Rest in Peace!

CHAPTER 9

Dilip Sardesai

by Rajdeep Sardesai

The stadium was swaying to the rhythm of foot tapping music. You could have been in Sao Paolo, Barcelona, Manchester, Munich, the great homes of football. But this was Fatorda stadium in Margao, a sleepy town in Goa that would awaken only to the sights and sounds of the beautiful game.

FC Goa was playing Delhi Dynamos in the Indian Soccer League, the glitzy equivalent of cricket's billion dollar baby, the Indian Premier League. 25,000 raucous Goans had crammed into every corner of the stadium. Sitting next to me was the sports minister of Goa who would leap with delight every time a player from the home side lashed out at goal. I was introduced to the minister as, "This is Rajdeep Sardesai sir, TV personality and son of Dilip Sardesai." "Ah, you are son of Dilip saab, he is our very own pride of Goa. Great man, but you know this is land of football, not cricket. Here, we kick the ball first, then learn how to hit it!"

Goa: India's smallest state by area, fourth smallest by population. To the outside world, Goa is defined in rather exotic terms as the country's tourist capital, home to sandy beaches, warm waters, bars and shacks, alcohol and soft drugs. The lure of the "good times" draws lakhs of domestic and foreign visitors to Goa's tranquil shores.

*Rajdeep Sardesai (aged three) with father Dilip in 1968
(Photo courtesy Rajdeep Sardesai)*

To most Goans their state is a prisoner of an image trap: the bohemian paradise is actually a conservative folk society, defined by a spirit of communidade, a Portuguese term for tightly knit village communities. The Portuguese withdrew from Goa in 1961 after more than 400 years of colonization, but Goan society still revolves around village panchayats: the idyllic beauty of nature is matched by a sense of relatively serene communal harmony with church spires and village temples happily co-existing across the skyline.

The long years of Portuguese rule influenced Goa in several ways, including its sporting interests. For the large Catholic community in particular – around 30 per cent of Goa – football was a sport that defined their identity, almost as if the sport connected the Goan Catholic to the wider Portuguese colonial diaspora from Rio to Lisbon.

Amidst swaying palm trees and lush green rice fields, the football ground was a space for young Goans to express themselves, to spin dreams of following in the footsteps of their idols from other lands, be it a Pele, Maradona, or in more recent times, a Ronaldo and a Messi.

Into this football crazy world stepped in Dilip Sardesai who, even after nearly 300 cricketers have represented the country in Tests, remains India's only Goan-born cricketer.

Goa in 1940 was still under the firm embrace of the Portuguese. Margao was its trading and commercial heartland, but still relatively tiny with a population of just around 50,000. The Sardesais were a typical middle class family, part of the town's influential Gowd Saraswat Brahmin community. The Saraswats are a small fish-eating Brahmin group along the west coast of India who trace their origins to the River Saraswati in the Himalayas: legend has it that when the river dried, there was large scale migration of the Saraswats to different parts of the country, including to the Konkan coastline, across Maharashtra, Goa and Karnataka. "We even fought in Shivaji's army and had been awarded a large tract of land," claimed my father's elder brother Anand when I met him to trace the family history.

Whether they were Shivaji's warriors or not, the sense is that the Sardesais by the 1940s had very little left of any land, wealth or privilege. My grandfather Narayan was an insurance agent while his mother Saraswati was raising a large family, and like many women of that generation seemed to spend a substantial part of her life in and out of maternity homes. The extended Sardesai family lived in a joint family home with several cousins and uncles. "We could have put up two cricket teams of just the Sardesai men in the house," my uncle Anand told me. The family wasn't wealthy but there was always enough food on the table, especially fish, which in Goa is staple diet. My father was the fifth child in a family of six, the youngest of the men in the house, and possibly the most pampered. He would often visit his elder sister's home in the neighbouring village of Kurpe, climb palm trees, pluck mangoes and jackfruits and swim in the river. My uncle Anand was a freedom-fighter, part of the guerilla-like groups who were taking on the Portuguese in their battle to liberate Goa. "I would be in and out of jail, but made sure that Dilip who was much younger than me would be kept away from any trouble," he says.

Like for many middle class families, education was seen as the ultimate weapon of survival. My father was sent to the local New Era School in Margao where studying Portuguese was mandatory and English was the medium of instruction after Class Four. While football was the main sport in school, there were a handful of boys, mainly from the Saraswat community, who also played cricket. They included my father's cousins, one of whom Sopan would go on to represent Bombay University. On the way to school was the Margao market where outside a nimbu pani shop, a tailor Narayan 'Master' would sit with a sowing machine. The tailor loved cricket and would become my father's first window to the game, showing him paper clippings of Indian Test cricketers and telling him stories of Vijay Merchant and Vijay Hazare, the champion batsmen of the era. "Narayan 'Master' introduced me to the game and gave me my first bat," my father told me. Many years later, when my father was playing a Test match in Mumbai, he invited Narayan to watch the game and to see the big city. It was his way to repay an old debt.

Like many of his generation, my father had no formal cricket coaching as a schoolboy, no visual imagery of cricket on television to emulate, no proper cricket kit. There was no cricket ground in Margao at the time but a large empty field behind the railway tracks was a space for the young to go and play. Margao didn't even have a turf wicket but only a makeshift matting pitch. "I just liked the idea of holding the bat in hand and hitting the ball hard. The faster the bigger boys bowled, the harder I hit them," was my father's explanation as to how he was initiated into the sport. The first time his family realized that young Sardesai might have a special skill was when a team of the Reserve Bank of India from Mumbai came to Margao in 1955 to play a local game. "Dilip scored a hundred in that game as a fifteen year old. That evening, the opposition captain came and told me that we should send him to Mumbai if we wanted him to become a better player," uncle Anand tells me. My father was finishing school that year and going to Mumbai for college and cricket seemed a natural progression.

In 1956, my father along with his parents and elder brothers left his beloved Goa for Mumbai. Migration for work is part of the Goan way of life: thousands of Goans even now travel to Mumbai and beyond to seek employment and fortune. Years later, my father would tell me how much he missed the joys of his childhood in Goa, the fish and the mangoes, the palm trees and the paddy fields. But in 1956, there was another dream that my father was living that had taken him away from his home. It was the great Indian dream, one that would be shared by many others from different parts of the country. Over the years, cricket and cinema have drawn many Indians from the small towns to the big cities in search of their golden rainbow. My father was chasing his own personal ambition: "It wasn't as if I was aspiring to play for India or anything, I just wanted to play cricket, I was in love with the game"

My father arrived to the bright lights of Mumbai in early 1956. Five years later, the teenager from Goa, who had never seen or played on a proper cricket ground as a schoolboy was playing for the country. This was the Nehruvian India of five year planning. But there was little planning in the incredible rise of a young man from the colonial outpost of Goa to the centre-stage of Indian cricket, only plenty of hard work, dedication, lots of talent, and yes, a bit of luck. Years later, I would ask my father to explain the secret of his almost instant success. "I guess I was hungry," he said, pointing to his now expanded mid-riff, "I just wanted it very badly."

It wasn't easy though. Indian cricket in the 1950s, like many aspects of society, was still trapped in its feudal origins. In a universe of elite clubs and princely patrons, Dilip Sardesai didn't have any godfather or benefactor. "When I came to Mumbai, I knew no one except my cousin Sopan who was a good cricketer and had already begun to play for Bombay University, I am a purely self-made cricketer," he later told me.

The family settled down in the Chowpatty beach area in south Mumbai in a building, Marina Mansion, that overlooked the Arabian Sea. The Chowpatty area was, and still is, a predominantly Gujarati neighbourhood, known for its excellent ice cream parlours and vegetarian food. The Gujaratis had been amongst the early converts to cricket, the seemingly leisurely pace of the game suiting a community not known for participating in physical activity. If Mahatma Gandhi was the Gujarati from Kathiawar who had galvanized a nation to freedom, Vijay Merchant, from a prominent Gujarati textile family of Mumbai, was arguably the first great Indian batsman and a role model for an entire generation. Merchant played his cricket at the Hindu Gymkhana, located at Marine Drive near Chowpatty. The Gymkhana grounds that dotted the sea face were a reminder of a period when cricket was organized along communal lines: Hindu, Islam and Parsee Gymkhana were cricket's early battlegrounds. "I saw Merchant bat once from a distance and was so excited that I didn't sleep that night and was just practising my defensive stroke with a bat in hand," my father said.

Dilip Sardesai first enrolled in Bhavans College, a stone's throw away from his home, and scored his first century in a college game. A year later, he had moved to Wilson College, a bigger, more prestigious college in the same area. A college with a rich history which counted then finance minister Morarji Desai amongst its alumni, it was in Wilson College that my father got his first big break. The college had a ground along the sea face and my father would go there every evening to play cricket and carrom, his other great sporting interest. One day, the team was short of one player and my father volunteered to fill the last spot. He took two catches and scored 25 not out, enough to impress the coach MS Naik. If a tailor on a street in Margao had initiated a young boy into the sport, an elderly coach in Mumbai would help him graduate to the next level. Naik spent hours with his ward, perfecting his skill and technique. "He was my first guru, I lost my father within a year of coming to Mumbai and Naik sir became a father figure to me," recalled my father.

When he wasn't at the college ground, Dilip Sardesai would practice on the terrace of his building. In the monsoon months, he would get the other boys in the area to throw a wet tennis ball at him to improve his reflexes. "We would bowl and Dilip would bat till late in the night under the lights on the terrace," recalls Mayuresh, a neighbor. The terrace training taught my father a useful lesson imbibed by the batsmen of that generation: keep hitting the ball along the ground to avoid getting out.

"It was on the terrace that I perfected the art of batting straight because if I hit the ball in the air, then I had to go down four floors to get the ball and then climb up again!" my father explained. The wet tennis ball practice would also become part of the informal coaching manual of many an Indian batsmen of the future.

The rigorous training began to pay off: in his two years at Wilson College, my father piled up the runs and slowly began to get noticed. In 1958, he played a game for his college against a strong Hindu Gymkhana side that included several Ranji Trophy players who were representing the Mumbai team. The team was led by Vinoo Mankad, who like Merchant, was an iconic figure in Indian cricket at the time, and perhaps the greatest spinning all-rounder the country has produced. Sardesai scored 90 not out in a score of 120, enough to make Mankad believe that he had seen a special talent.

That evening, Mankad came to the dressing room and told my father, "Beta, I am making you a member of the Gymkhana, from now on, you will play for us. Don't worry about the fees; I will take care of it!" Vinoobhai, as my father called him endearingly, would become a benefactor for life.

The high scores in college cricket meant that Sardesai was ready to take his next step: in 1958, he was picked for the Bombay University team for the first time. Over the next three years, he would dominate university cricket as part of a powerful Mumbai side, scoring centuries and double centuries almost at will. Mumbai was becoming a dominant force in Indian cricket with the emerging Maharashtrian middle class the engine of its success. Names like Ajit Wadekar, Ramakant Desai, Bapu Nadkarni were part of this mini-cricket revolution being stirred in the maidans of Mumbai. Through the late 1950s and the decade of the 1960s, Mumbai would be to cricket what Bengal was for a long time to football: a nursery of the sport. Between the golden period of 1958 to 1973, the Mumbai team never lost the Ranji Trophy. In fact, my father has a unique record: he was never on a losing Ranji Trophy side!

When India won a Test series in 1971 in England for the first time, the team had six Mumbai players, my father one of them. University cricket provided the platform for the rise of Mumbai as a cricket powerhouse. "It was great fun," recalled my father, "We were all very young, and would crisscross the country by train, mostly in second class, playing cards and singing songs."

Cricket wasn't just fun, it also provided employment. His father having passed away suddenly, Sardesai needed a job. In that period, public sector banks and the House of Tatas were the few companies who would employ sportsmen. One Tata group company was Associated Cement Company (ACC) whose chief talent scout and general manager was Madhav Mantri, a former Test cricketer and also uncle of the legendary Sunil Gavaskar.

Mantri had seen the young Sardesai bat in a club match between Hindu Gymkhana and his own club, Dadar Union, and it was literally a case of love at first sight! "The very first day I saw him play I knew he would play for India, there was no doubt in my mind," he told me. Mantri, who would become another father figure, offered Sardesai a job in ACC for the princely sum of Rs. 1200 in the purchase department. "I didn't really have to do anything much. I would clock into work at 9 am, and by 2 pm leave for the ground for practice!" my father recalled.

The biggest break though would come soon after as Sardesai was picked for the trials for the Combined Universities team to play the visiting Pakistanis in the winter of 1960. "I went to the trials and there were dozens of boys who seemed much bigger than me. I wasn't sure that I would get a chance," my father told me. He needn't have worried.

The chief selector at the time was Lala Amarnath, another larger than life figure in post 1947 Indian cricket. The first Indian to score a test century on his debut in 1933, Lala's cricketing career had been celebrated and controversial: he had been sent back home from the Indian cricket team touring England in 1936 after he got into a fight with the Maharaja of Vizianagaram. But Lala was an astute talent spotter, someone who believed in meritocracy and calling a spade a shovel. He saw Sardesai play a perfect defensive shot in the trials and called him aside, "Look son, I am going to pick you in the team, but I don't know about these other selectors, some of whom who don't know the .ABC of technique. *Thoda ek do ball hawa mein maro* (hit one or two balls in the air), they will be happy. The rest you leave to me!" A few lofted shots later, my father found himself in the Combined Universities team to play Pakistan.

Sardesai didn't miss his opportunity. He scored 87 in that game against Pakistan, was picked for a Board President's XI team where he scored a century and then was made 12th man for the Test match that followed.

Less than a year later in December 1961, he was lining up to make his Test debut against England at the age of 21, shaking hands with Jawaharlal Nehru at the Feroze Shah Kotla grounds in Delhi. He was introduced to Nehru as a "young man who hails from Goa." The prime minister looked at him and smiled, "Ah Goa! Don't worry, the Indian army will soon liberate your state!"

On December 17, 30,000 Indian ground troops marched into Goa. Two days later, Goa had been freed of Portuguese rule. While Goa celebrated freedom, Dilip Sardesai was rejoicing too: he had just become the 103rd player to wear an India cap. "The first day I got the cap, I went to sleep wearing it, I was so excited!" he told me. From the paddy fields of Margao to the cricket stadiums of India, it had been a remarkable journey.

Indeed, the images of his beloved Goa would stay with him for life. In 1971 in the West Indies, he had his finest moment for India while scoring 642 runs in the series. I asked him what he enjoyed most about playing cricket in the Caribbean. "You know, the West Indies is just like Goa, the sea breeze, the beaches, yes, even the rum is like our feni!" he laughed. That was Dilip Sardesai for you: Goan heart, Indian soul!

Rajdeep on Rajdeep:

Senior journalist and author, desperately wanted to emulate his father and play for India but eventually realized that nepotism doesn't work on the cricket field. Nor does talent run in the blood. So settled for a life in journalism and has been a print and television journalist for over three decades. Yet, prized cricket achievements include captaining Bombay schools and also scoring 66 not out on first class debut for Oxford University against a strong Kent side that included Derek Underwood who announced his retirement soon after the game. Also played for Combined British Universities against the touring Pakistanis in 1987 but was bowled by Abdul Qadir for just a single run. That's when realized it was time to pack bags and discover a life beyond the boundary. Has written books on elections and cricket, the difference being that politics isn't played with a straight bat! His cricket book, Democracy's XI: The Great Story of Indian Cricket was shortlisted as the MCC Cricket Book of the Year.

CHAPTER 10

Tiger Pataudi

by Ramesh Sharma

My first glimpse of Tiger Pataudi was at his home at 1 Dupleix Road in New Delhi. I had gone there to meet his actor wife, the glamorous Sharmila Tagore, who was the female lead of my film *New Delhi Times* opposite Shashi Kapoor. I had to discuss some shooting dates with her and their domestic had ushered me to the drawing room. Like all Lutyens Zone bungalows, there is little daylight in the inner rooms of these houses. The semi-darkened room seemed that much more sombre because of the sound of silence enveloping it.

And sitting alone in that tastefully appointed room, with every kind of conversation piece strewn around, I heard faint footsteps and saw a silhouette of a man in his kurta pyjama peep in and then walk away. It was Sharmila's husband Mansur Ali Khan Pataudi. He didn't greet me or even acknowledge my presence. We had not yet been introduced and I must confess I was a trifle intimidated. As if I had trespassed into his privacy. Just then Sharmila walked and greeted me with her warm dimpled smile, asked me if I wanted tea and put me at ease.

A few years later I met Tiger again, this time accompanied by ITC executives and the executives of an advertising firm. I had been engaged by them to produce and direct a video – *The Wills Video of Excellence – The History of One Day Cricket*. We had a list of possible anchors for the film.

But I wanted someone with a camera presence, who could speak impeccable English and more importantly had both the gravitas and credibility. The obvious choice was Tiger Pataudi. And Mudar Patherya, who was writing the script with me, was equally enthusiastic about this selection. It helped that Mudar was working with Tiger in *Sportsworld*, a magazine Pataudi edited.

Ramesh Sharma (second from left) with Sunil Gavaskar and Tiger Pataudi Caption (Photo courtesy Ramesh Sharma)

Those days we had no teleprompters. So I explained to Pataudi that we would shoot his pieces to the camera in the front lawn of his house and he would have to memorize the lines, but deliver them as if he was ad-libbing. He had a wry smile," So you want me to compete with my wife?" We all laughed a little louder than necessary at this weak joke.

To Pataudi's credit, though he struggled the first few days with his on-camera performance, he was professional enough to hear out my critique and by the third day, he delivered his lines perfectly on the very first or second take.

The 1987 Reliance World Cup was being played in India and Pakistan, and we took the opportunity to get interviews with some of the luminaries of one-day cricket. To be able to get a ringside view of the changes as the game of cricket evolved.

Very soon we realised that almost all of these international cricketers agreed readily to be part of my film, partly because they were being paid, but mainly because Tiger Pataudi was interviewing them.

Imran Khan, for instance, agreed to come to Pataudi's home for the interview. But we had to drive to Jaipur to get Vivian Richards where the West Indies were playing a World Cup match. Our co-ordinator had managed to get Richards for the next day and he had agreed to come to our hotel for the shoot

The evening before we were having dinner at the Rambagh Palace Hotel and a few tables away Richards was there with some of his teammates. After a while I saw him walk towards our table and I told Tiger that Richards was coming towards us. Richards greeted Pataudi very tentatively, addressing him throughout as 'sir'. Tiger introduced us to him. Then in a hesitant but polite manner Richards asked Tiger if we could push the filming of his interview from 10 am next morning to 12 noon. Without even a beat or allowing the question to sink in, Tiger looked up to Richards and said," No. I have other commitments so let us keep it for 10 am." I drew a sharp breath and you could cut through the tension in the air with a butter knife, because of the curt tone Tiger had used.

Richards laughed sheepishly, regretting he had even dared broach the subject," No problem sir", he said, ''I will be there at 10". I looked at Pataudi, after Richards had left and asked him, why was he so rude to that man? We had no other shoot, we could have easily accommodated him at 12 noon. Tiger replied: "He had agreed for 10 am. Don't see any reason why he should want to change it at the last moment." The crew was apprehensive that Richards would probably cancel the shoot. But to our relief, he was at our hotel at 10 sharp and we got a interview full of wonderful insights.

It was only then I came to understand the awe and respect Tiger commanded from the new generation of cricket legends, long after he had retired from the game.

As a cricket lover growing up in the Himalayan town of Kalimpong, studying in Darjeeling, where, with no talent for the game itself but only a passion for it, which by itself was not enough to get myself selected for the playing XI, I 'Walter Mittyed' out my fantasies vicariously, standing in as an umpire in the local Edinburgh Shield cricket matches.

Those days, there was no television and our heroes were brought to us by the magic of radio commentary. Marshall McLuhan the Canadian philosopher called radio a 'hot medium' because we were spoon-fed the content. And so the ball by ball commentary of the likes of Suresh Saraiya, Pearson Surita (whose brother Ivan incidentally was the Commissioner in the Jalpaiguri Division and had a house in Kalimpong and boasted he was the Nabob of Uttar Bangla,), Berry Sarbadhikary, Richie Benaud, John Arlott to name a few from that era, with their language skill and technical knowledge of the game, created the narratives for us. They helped us share the pulsating excitement and put us right in the middle of the field with the players.

Thus the majesty of Mansur Ali Khan Pataudi's cricketing talent was first brought to me by the description of his shots and fielding through radio commentary.

Tiger was imbued with a glamour that came partly from his pedigree but mostly by how he led from the front. A born leader, he had captained his school team Winchester in the UK, where in a bit of irony, which gave him great satisfaction, he enjoyed narrating, that he beat the record set by Douglas Jardine for the maximum runs scored in a season. It was under Jardine that Tiger's father, the Senior Pataudi had toured Australia as member of the English team, in the notorious Bodyline series. So disgusted was the senior Nawab of Pataudi by Jardine's tactics, that he refused the captain's orders.

His royal lineage, his Oxford pedigree, the fact that he was the first Indian to captain the Oxford team added to Tiger's aura.

Then the tyranny of fate intervened. One uneventful night in 1961, Pataudi, instead of walking 300 yards to his hotel, after an evening meal, chose to ride along in his friend's Morris Minor car, which met with a freak accident. An accident where Pataudi lost the vision in his right eye. This made Pataudi's myth that much more heroic. Because instead of swaddling in self-pity and retiring from the game, Pataudi went back to the nets to practice. His passion for cricket remained intact and fierce.

And this gave birth to a profile in courage, as he returned to first- class cricket with impaired vision in one eye and a damaged shoulder. Only six months after the accident, Pataudi made his Test debut playing against England in Delhi in December 1961. He scored 103 in the Third Test in Madras, his second, helping India to its first series win against England. As he once told me, he felt he lost 30-40 per cent of his ability as a batsman due to his eye injury. But with whatever he retained he played exquisite, entertaining cricket.

Tiger Pataudi was sometimes modest about his own feats. In his book Tiger's Tale, he self effacingly wrote, "In the land of the blind, the one-eyed is the king." He was joking, because Tiger's contemporaries were the likes of Polly Umrigar, Abbas Ali Baig, ML Jaisimha, BS Chandrasekhar, Bishan Singh Bedi, Vijay Manjrekar, Dilip Sardesai, Nari Contractor, Chandu Borde and many others.

In the early days of Indian cricket, royalty and cricket were inextricably linked. There was Kumar Shri Ranjitsinhji, his nephew Duleepsinhji both classy cricketers. Then there was Maharaj Kumar of Vizianagaram, popularly called Vizzy, who was in the Indian XI only because he opened his purse strings and sponsored the team. But Tiger was the real deal. A regal lineage reinforced by prodigious talent and amplified with innate leadership qualities.

The cricket administrators recognised this and at the age of 21, in an effort to nurture him, he was chosen to be the vice-captain of the Indian team touring West Indies in 1962, led by Nari Contractor.

The lethal West Indies pace attack demolished the Indians in the first two Test matches. And in the game against Barbados, the brutal pace of Charlie Griffith, almost caused the death of Contractor who could not duck the bouncer. An emergency operation saved his life but ended his career. Contractor was flown back to India and on 23 March 1962, Mansur Ali Khan Pataudi became the youngest Test captain at the age of 21 years and 77 days.

It was as captain that Tiger made his mark. He moulded a team consisting of players from all parts of a country known for its immense diversity, into one that played, not as individuals from particular regions, but for the country.

His contemporaries still remember how Tiger made the dressing room buzz with this inclusive spirit. He chose his eleven and played to the strength of his best players. So it was under him that the likes of Prasanna, Chandrasekhar, Venkataraghavan and Bedi, were given chances time and again to prove their talent and these four emerged as among the most menacing spin bowlers in the history of cricket.

Although he was a private person and almost reticent, he wasn't above playing pranks. During our drive to Jaipur for discussing the script for the film, he regaled us with stories about how he and Madhav Rao Scindia, had Prasanna, Gundappa Viswanath and Chandrasekhar crying. They staged a mock dacoit kidnapping of Prasanna in Gwalior and the cricketers were convinced the dacoits were real and they would all be killed. Tiger had that rare guffaw as he described his terrified colleagues weeping for their lives.

Another time he said he put a dead alligator in the bed of his room-mate who came in at 4 am, slept with the alligator only to wake up screaming, shrieking next morning and trembling with fear. A scene right out of *The Godfather*!

It was under his captaincy that a killer instinct was first incubated and the Indian XI got its first series victory abroad when it defeated New Zealand 3-1 in 1968.

His career statistics may seem average, he scored 2,793 runs in the 46 test matches that he played, with six centuries, including 203 not out and the average of 34.91 and India won only nine of the 40 Test matches he captained.

But Pataudi was a dashing cricketer to watch, with his shirt collar up, his cap rakishly tilted covering the right eye as he walked into bat with a hint of a swagger. His impaired vision may have been a handicap to players with less talent but watching Tiger drive the ball gracefully through the covers, or loft it over the bowler's head, it was difficult to imagine he was handicapped with the loss of vision in one eye.

As Bill O'Reilly remarked: "His 75 and 85 in the Melbourne Test in 1967-68 where he played with a hamstring injury was remarkable because in effect he was playing with one good eye and one good leg." And he faced the most ferocious pace bowling, without helmets or face guards.

Tiger was also a remarkably agile fielder, almost feline as he prowled in the covers to save a run or catch the rising shot. Despite his physical handicap, he was the precursor to athletic fielding which has now become the hallmark of limited overs and T20 cricket.

Tiger strengthened the glamour of his princely pedigree and multiplied his charisma by marrying the heart throb of the Hindi film industry, Sharmila Tagore.

What makes Tiger Pataudi a permanent fixture in the pantheon of all-time greats of Indian cricket was not just his cricketing achievements but also the grace he displayed after retirement. He did not lobby for or ask to be part of the BCCI. He did not grudge the brashness of some of the upstarts of one-day cricket, for whom cricket was only a money making job.

Tiger told me that during his days the players were paid only Rs 2,000 per test match. But that didn't matter because he played the game, not for the money, but only for the passion and the love of the sport. With his passing away on September 22, 2011, cricket lost one of its authentic heroes, a role model and the last true Nawab of the gentleman's game.

Ramesh on Ramesh:

Like millions of Indians, has been a member of the unofficial selection committee that chooses the Indian cricket eleven for every match, though most of the time his selections are ignored. He has also served as a non-playing captain, sitting in front of his TV, advising batsmen how to play the ball and bowlers how to bowl, even though his own performance as a cricketer did not warrant his selection for the North Point College cricket XI in Darjeeling. He made up for all that by producing and directing the bestselling video The Wills Video of Excellence-The History of One Day Cricket hosted by Tiger Pataudi. He is also the only filmmaker who has the distinction of having directed the husband-wife couple of both Sharmila Tagore and Tiger Pataudi.

CHAPTER 11

ML Jaisimha

by PR Man Singh

The year 1953—my first glimpse of Motganhalli Laxminarsu Jaisimha was when he came to the Vehicle Sub-Depot grounds to play a league match for Marredpalli Cricket Club. Batting at No.3, the loud cheer that he received from his team mates as he entered the ground, made me wonder as to what was so great about this schoolboy.

As the years passed, I had the occasion of playing against him and also under his captaincy for Nizam College. I observed that what differentiated him from others was his batting with a very straight bat, which was also the reason for most of his drives being in the 'V'.

In a particular Behram-ud-Dowlah match, while playing for Nizam College against Deccan Blues at the Fateh Maidan Ground on a rain affected grass wicket — a 'sticky dog', his innings against the-then world's best off-spinner, Ghulam Ahmed, was simply outstanding. Watching him from the non-strikers end, I was awestruck at the ease with which he negotiated the bowling, while the other batsmen were jumping all over the place. This innings probably impressed the India captain (Ghulam) enough to introduce Jai to Lala Amarnath when he came down to coach the Hyderabad youngsters under the Raj Kumari Amrit Kaur coaching scheme, as a potential India batsman.

The other opportunity that I had of playing under his captaincy was when he led the Osmania University team in the Rohinton Baria Tournament. After the first match, Jai left for Ahmedabad to play against the visiting Australians. He had made his Test debut on the Indian team's tour of England in 1959 and was already a Test player when he traveled with us to Madras for the Inter University Tournament. We travelled second class by train in an unreserved compartment, slept on the floor of the University Union Pavilion at Egmore and Jai was with us all through as a member of the team. Never for once did he throw his weight around as a Test player or demand he be treated as one. This revealed a facet of his character —humility.

PR Man Singh (centre) with ML Jaisimha (left) and Tiger Pataudi (Photo courtesy PR Man Singh)

Since Jai was unable to represent the University (because of his India duty), the then Vice Chancellor of Osmania University suspended him. This affected his chances of selection and captaincy of the Combined Universities team which was to play a game against the visiting Australians. However, after much persuasion, Jai got selected and scored runs to stake a claim in the Indian team for the Calcutta Test, where he created a world record by batting on all the five days of the match.

Though Jai started as an opening batsman and also a new ball bowler, as he progressed in his career and got into the Test side, he did not like to open the innings. Unfortunately, the middle order hardly gave any scope for accommodation, being packed with big and established names like, Vijay Manjrekar, Polly Umrigar and Chandu Borde. The only place vacant was the opening slot. In the match against Pakistan at Kanpur, Jai opened and he batted for more than 500 minutes, scoring 99 runs before he was run out. This prompted the English '99 Club' to invite Jai to be their member. Despite such performances, Jai was frequently a victim of the selectors' whims and fancies and most of the time was at the receiving end.

During India's second Test match against West Indies in 1966-67, at Calcutta, the organizers had sold tickets beyond the seating capacity, which led to a riot. During the team meeting, Jai raised the issue of security to the team. This tale was carried by one of the team members to K. Datta Ray of the Cricket Association of Bengal, who was also the Chairman of the Selection Committee. Jai was promptly dropped from the XI for the next match at Madras, and in his anger, probably Jai ignored Datta Ray, who then ensured that Jai was not selected for the 1967 tour of England. Abbas Ali Baig too was dropped. That was the time when I had planned a tour of the Hyderabad Blues team to then-Ceylon.

On the tour Jai batted like a champion. In the match against their national side, Jai scored a century in the first innings and narrowly missed in the second, being run out on 97. If he had completed the second hundred also he would have been the first ever batsman from abroad to score a hundred in each innings in Ceylon. Jai had this natural gift of fighting and loads of determination.

On the eve of the Indian team's tour to Australia and New Zealand in 1967-68, there was a selection camp at Khadakwasla, near Pune, under Col Hemu Adhikari. Once again, Jai was left out by the selection committee, headed by Datta Ray.

Ghulam Sahib, who was the Manager of the touring team, was co-opted to the selection committee meeting. Apparently, during the meeting there was a lot of discussion about Jai's selection, and after long deliberation, Jai was included as one of the reserves/stand byes.

Before the team left for Australia, Ghulam Sahib instructed me to ensure that Jai kept in touch with his batting. I organized the practice nets for Jai at Gymkhana Grounds on a matting wicket and asked all the top pace bowlers of the city to be present and bowl to Jai. Sufficient new balls were provided and Jai was practicing in right earnestness.

BS Chandrasekhar's injury while on tour triggered Jai's call to join the team in Australia. As had been the practice in the past, Jai carried my bat with him and left for Australia. The Brisbane Test, which Jai played within a few days of his arrival, saw him score an epic 70 runs in the first innings following by a brilliant century in the second. The Australian media was left wondering as to how a player of such calibre was dropped in the first place. Sadly, Jails performance on the rest of the tour was nothing much to write home about.

It was shocking for me when Jai was sacked as the captain of the South Zone team and in his place S. Venkataraghavan was appointed for the Duleep Trophy in 1971. Being extremely hurt and upset, Jai wanted to retire from first-class cricket. It was then that I had a long chat with him and impressed upon him that he should participate in the Duleep Trophy and perform well to not only convey that captaincy was not all that he was interested in but also that he was a batsman of a different class altogether.

Eventually Jai agreed to my suggestion and the gritty and determined cricketer he was, he played and scored a century against Central Zone in the quarter-finals and followed it up with another one in the final against East Zone.

These performances got him a berth for the West Indies tour in 1971. On this tour, he was more of a mentor to the young Sunil Gavaskar and was also a hands-on guide to the skipper Ajit Wadekar. His gritty partnership with Sunny during the last Test at Port of Spain helped India draw the match and win the series. That was the last time that he donned India colours. Jai did attempt to make a comeback and the best chance for him to do so was against West Indies when they toured India in 1974-75.

Once again, the only place in the playing XI was the opener's slot. Jai and I had a long discussion on this and I suggested that he should open the innings for South Zone when they were to play against the Windies at Hyderabad, score runs and stake a claim for a place. Initially Jai agreed and also practiced very seriously on a cement wicket against all the pace bowlers of Hyderabad. However, on the day of the match, he declined to open the innings. He probably felt that he would be unable to negotiate the pace and swing of the Windies quicks — Keith Boyce, Andy Roberts and Bernard Julian. This put the final seal on his India career.

Jai's leadership qualities were known to all but he was unlucky never to lead India. Probably, Pataudi's elevation to that post was rather early and also he became the captain at a time when circumstances were beyond anyone's control. Also, all through Jai's cricketing career, it was happening all the time that juniors like Wadekar and Venkataraghavan were getting the job. This is where my belief in destiny gets stronger.

I had the privilege of having Jai travel with the Hyderabad Blues team on tours abroad. On these tours whenever I asked Jai to lead the side, he would politely decline but was always available when I sought his advice on the field. He was a very important member of the touring party and made a lot of friends. He toured with the Blues to Ceylon in 1967, to East Africa in 1971, to Australia and Fiji Islands in 1973 and West Indies in 1975.

On the last tour, even Pataudi was in the team. Jai would play very serious cricket on the field and used to enjoy himself and have fun off it. A man of great cricketing talent and determination and also a keen student of the game, perhaps Jai's only weakness was that whenever he said that he was fit and raring to go, he would fail on that day. In contrast, the times when he said he was unwell and not fully fit, God alone help the opponents on that day!

All along our 40 years of friendship and association, there was only one occasion, when we had our differences — when he contested along with me for the Hon. Secretary's post of the Hyderabad Cricket Association. He had been misled by some of his other close friends and associates that after Ghulam Ahmed, who was a Test cricketer, in all fitness of things, only another Test player should take over the responsibility. Everyone, including myself, acknowledged Jai as a great cricketer, but cricket administration was a different cup of tea and Jai was not cut out for that. I won the election and soon after we were back to our old friendship.

My promises to Jai that I would ensure he became a national selector and also that I would conduct a benefit game for him were fulfilled. When an opportunity arose, I also backed him to be the manager of the Indian team on one of its tours abroad. I fulfilled all these commitments made to him and he was also very appreciative of my efforts.

I have very fond memories and always cherish my friendship with Jai and all the memorable years spent in his company. It is sad that he could not do more for Hyderabad cricket due to his untimely demise in July 1999 at the age of 60. Destiny was against him and Hyderabad was deprived of his talents off the field. RIP dear friend.

Man Singh on Man Singh:

A fixture on the Hyderabad cricket scene for over six decades. Forever known as the manager of the victorious 1983 Prudential World Cup team. Also deputy manager on the historic 1978 tour of Pakistan. Author of the fragrant history of Hyderabad cricket, Cricket Biryani and of other books too. And a first-class cricketer to boot!

CHAPTER 12

Mohinder Amarnath

by Karthik Venkatesh

It hurts to remember the humiliation. Even today.
The 1982 Asian Games hockey final between India and Pakistan was a nightmare that I can never seem to forget. The 7-1 defeat that India suffered was a complete humiliation, of course. I made it a lot worse for myself by insisting on watching it to the bitter end even as I shed tears of utter despair and helplessness.

Bangalore was still a sleepy little town then. It broke for two-hour lunch breaks at one in the afternoon, went to bed at seven in the evening and its weekends began on Friday at around three. In hindsight, excitement seemed in short supply. But it all seemed perfectly fine since we didn't know any better.

When I shed those tears, I was two months shy of my eighth birthday. Television and live telecasts were a new and important aspect of the demure lives that the world I inhabited led, because suddenly, everything became very exciting.

And then the humiliation.

Nothing could quite compensate for it.

Not the fact that Chand Ram, Kaur Singh, Charles Borromeo and others were being celebrated for their gold-winning athletic performances. Not the fact that the Indian contingent had earned a record-breaking 13 gold medals.

Nothing.

Mohinder Amarnath in the Good Morning India studio with Gulu in 1999. (Gulu Ezekiel Collection)

I did not know it then. But amidst all the gloom, an unlikely hero was to emerge a few weeks later who would change my life forever.

Previously, hockey and cricket had competed for my attention. Hockey was India's national sport, or so I was told, and a sport in which India had won many Olympic gold medals. So, stick and bat were both equally important.

The Asian Games humiliation forced me to turn in cricket's direction to recover.

The hero who helped seven-year-old me deal with the pain was MohinderAmarnath. And his claim to fame was that he had stood tall and unvanquished against a rampaging Imran Khan in the six Tests that India and Pakistan played in late 1982 and early 1983. India lost the series 3-0. But Mohinder made it seem more bearable.

I heaved a sigh of relief. All was not lost. Men of steel still walked the face of the earth.

A few weeks later, against the thundering pacemen of the West Indies, Mohinder carried on in much the same vein. He stood up to the quicks and made it all look so easy. India lost that series 2-0. But Mohinder made it bearable. Again.

Then came the Prudential Cup of 1983. India had an unbelievable run. And before I could come to terms with it, India was in the final. The final, of course, is a milestone of sorts. It marks the day that Indian cricket and in the fullness of time, world cricket, changed forever. And Mohinder was in the thick of it. Batting sensibly, bowling brilliantly and then, picking up the last wicket and sprinting away, face lit up with the joy of victory.

It was the most glorious time of my boyhood. India were world champions and my hero was in the thick of it, making it all happen.

Close to four decades later, I can still feel that quivering sliver of excitement as if it had happened just yesterday.

What prompted this curious turn of events and resulted in my choosing this cricketer in particular? Surely, there were others whom I could have chosen. What prompted the decision was a prosaic turn of events.

The two brothers who lived next door and with whom I played most of my cricket in the common compound had laid claim to Gavaskar and Kapil respectively. I had to choose from the others. That's how things were in the boyhood stakes in my neck of the woods. We booked our heroes and did not allow others to claim them.

Sandip Patil was definitely in the reckoning. His successes in the 1982 England series did catch my eye, but I wasn't quite ready to commit myself. I needed a proven performer. He was flashy, reckoned my father, and then added that flashiness was both good and bad. On his day, he could be a world-beater, but such days were rare.

Thus was my mind made up. I needed someone who could truly measure up to Gavaskar and Kapil. The need was for someone whose sheer consistency would guarantee that there would never be more than the odd rainy day as far as his performance went.

Mohinder's initial success in that 1982-83 Pakistan series helped. Quite promptly, I proclaimed that he was my favourite. It was a childish leap of faith. There was no cricketer then who could match Gavaskar and Kapil in the consistency stakes. That was Indian cricket's biggest bugbear back then. Many flattered, only to deceive.

But miracle of miracles, Mohinder did not let me down. He won my trust and faith through sheer performance. Match after match over the next several months, he performed. My prayers had been answered. It was as if I had chosen and he had delivered, only to please me.

I now had to do my bit. To underline my devotion, I promptly proceeded to imitate him. I batted left-handed and imitating his crouching batting stance wasn't quite so simple, but I managed to get it right, after a string of scores in the 0-5 range. Devotion was clearly hard and humiliating work. But I wasn't prepared to go down without a fight. His leisurely bowling run-up, on the other hand, was much easier to imitate. That was a relief.

Over the next five years, through thick and thin, I remained devoted to my idol. It was the least I could do as payback for those many months of unbridled joy.

As it turned out, his successes in 1982-83 did not quite herald a new dawn. In late 1983, when the West Indies toured India for a six-test series, some months after getting the short end of the stick in the Prudential Cup, Mohinder had a horrendous time. His scores mirrored my own when I had decided to imitate his stance. It must surely rank as among the greatest cricket meltdowns ever witnessed.

Predictably, Mohinder was promptly dropped for some time. He came back and then was dropped again. And came back yet again, before in 1988, he was dropped for the last time and then with uncharacteristic fury, labelled the selectors a 'bunch of jokers' and vanished from the national scene, this time forever. This was pretty much how things had been for most of his career. Or so I was told. But for eight-year-olds, history is bunk. What mattered was a match, a performance and a series. As far as I was concerned, Mohinder had earned it by being there for me when I needed a hero.

In retrospect, my choice of Mohinder was rather odd. He wasn't the 'Rock of Gibraltar' that Gavaskar was or the swashbuckling buccaneer that Kapil was. He was 'Old Faithful', a sheepish character who didn't quite stand out as say a Sandip Patil could sometimes do. But, pressure had forced my hand. I needed someone who could measure upto Kapil and Gavaskar. When the three of us discussed performances, I needed someone who could stand shoulder to shoulder with the two dominant figures of Indian cricket then.

For that annus mirabilis of my life (and his too, I imagine), it was Mohinder!

Karthik on Karthik :

Too timid to play cricket at any level. So coped with this trauma by reading about the sport instead. In time, that helped in editing many cricket books and thereby live a vicarious cricketing life.

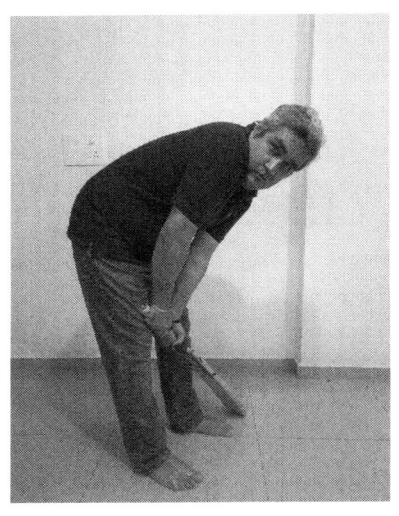

Karthik Venkatsh (Photo courtesy Karthik Venkatesh)

An editor with Westland Books and oversees Westland Sport, their sports imprint. Still believes has an outside chance at playing 'propah' cricket ... at least for a local club! This dream refuses to die.

EPILOGUE
Ode to Heroes
by Gulu Ezekiel

Bishan Singh Bedi

To A Legend On His 70Th Birthday (2016)

Bishan, silent killer with the ball
Chuckling quietly as one by one they fall.

Gentle executioner, they called you
A spin wizard, thru and thru.

Weaver of dreams, here you stand
A poet with red cherry in hand.

Not white or pink for you, only red
That beautiful arc, leaving batsmen stranded with feet of lead.

Flights of fancy, luring them to their doom
Like a spider to a fly, cramped for room.

Like a vision in white, you appear in a dream
No finer sight on a cricket field has ever been seen.

Lion of Punjab, you call a spade a shovel!
No fear in your heart
Now the seventh decade of your life you start.

Yes, Bish you turn 70 today
But for millions of cricket lovers around the world, you remain immortal

Gulu with Bishan Singh Bedi at the Feroze Shah Kotla, Delhi during the Board President's XI vs. Australians in March 2001. (Photo by Mark Ray).

BS Chandrasekhar

The modest match winner

Chandra, the smiling assassin
Deadly with ball in hand
Off the field, none gentler than this gentle man.

Googly, wrong un, top-spinner.
India's greatest all-time match winner.

Polio withered his wiry right hand
Like a whiplash would make the ball land.

Charging in with brutal intent
Now with age, all passion spent.

At Brabourne, Oval, Port-of-Spain, MCG
Chandra in his pomp for all to see.

It was in the summer of 1971
That he had the Poms hopping and on the run.

'Chandra, Chandra, Chandra' the Oval crowd chanted
A famous victory his legendary bowling granted.

Even the mighty Viv turned to 'keeper Kiri in horror
'Quicker than Thommo is your master bowler."

Childhood trauma, setbacks, accidents he suffered
But Chandra, you braveheart you kept smiling, never demurred!

Lover of Mukesh's melodious tunes
When will we see the like of the magnificent Chandra again?

GR Vishvanath

The Pocket Dynamo

Vishy, the wristy maestro, Little Big Man
Indian cricket's most beloved across this vast land

It all started at Green Park in the winter of '69
In the first innings came a zero
but in the second you become our hero

Twenty-five boundaries peppered that glorious 137 and you never looked back
To the bowlers throughout your career you took the

attack

That square cut hit like a whiplash
In a jiffy to the fence the ball would crash

The late cut, delicate as a summer breeze
Hit with such precision, the fielders would suddenly freeze

Green Park, Eden, Chepauk, Christchurch, Port of Spain, MCG...
Another like you the cricket world will never see.

When captain in the 1980 Bombay Golden Jubilee Test
You showed India at its glorious best

England's Bob Taylor you did recall
Even though it meant that India would fall

Two glorious innings against the rampaging
Andy Roberts you did play
Never again will we see such as this we did say.

With wrists of hardened steel and a heart of solid gold
the nation's imagination for over a decade did you hold

Modesty thy middle name
But success did not go to your head, nor fame

Vishy, you bloody beauty!

Tiger Pataudi

The Prince of Indian Cricket

Tiger, Tiger burning bright
Our beloved skipper who never gave up the fight

Pataudi, Pat, Mansur, Nawab or Tiger they called you
But really, what's in a name?
The prince of tiny Pataudi, the king of a mighty game

Records and runs flowed from your bat when young
Then came the accident that shocked and stung

Months later you were back with just one good eye
A century in your third Test much to our delight

Another accident this time, to Contractor
and suddenly you found yourself elevated to skipper

Pride, passion and love for the nation
Your commitment to the cause brought Indian cricket great ovation

That gallant 148 at Leeds guided the rocking ship steadily
No wonder they dubbed you the Nawab of Headingley!

Then months later it was at the MCG
two mighty innings despite a leg injury

Proud son of a proud father, who stood up to Jardine
India's finest captain by a country mile!

Your death left a huge void in our hearts
But from our memory you will never depart

EAS Prasanna

The canny offie

Pras, the portly sweaty hangman,

Tossing the ball up as if on an invisible rope.

Just as the batsman would step up to drive,

Seemingly came a gentle tug...the poor guy really had no hope!

Was it sorcery, illusionism or just something out of the blue?

The batsman, the fielders, the 'keeper, none of us really knew.

No doosra, no teesra, just the master of flight and spin,

With those tricks in your bag, how many Tests you helped India win.

The Kiwis and the Kangaroos you foxed and had them on the hop

As that tantalizing floater would suddenly dip and drop

Batsmen with twinkling footwork like Chappell you loved to bowl to

The best offie they ever played of you they said so

Elder statesman of the legendary quartet of spin

Memories of watching the master at work will never dim.

Printed in Great Britain
by Amazon